Conversations with Carl Henry:
Christianity for Today

Conversations with Carl Henry: Christianity for Today

Carl F.H. Henry

Volume 18
Symposium Series

The Edwin Mellen Press
Lewiston/Queenston

Library of Congress Cataloging-in-Publication Data

Henry, Carl Ferdinand Howard, 1913-
  Conversations with Carl Henry.

  (Symposium series ; v. 18)
  1. Evangelicalism--Miscellanea. 2. Theology--
Miscellanea. 3. Henry, Carl Ferdinand Howard,
1913- --Interviews. I. Title. II. Series:
Symposium series (Edwin Mellen Press) ; v. 18.
BR1640.H39   1986   230'.044'0924   86-666
ISBN 0-88946-709-9 - Hardcover
ISBN 0-88946-711-0 - Soft cover

> This is volume 18 in the continuing series
> Symposium Series
> Volume 18 ISBN 0-88946-709-9
> SS Series ISBN 0-88946-989-X

Copyright© 1986 Carl F.H. Henry

All rights reserved. For information contact

The Edwin Mellen Press   The Edwin Mellen Press
P.O. Box 450   P.O. Box 67
Lewiston, New York   Queenston, Ontario
USA 14092   CANADA L0S 1L0

Printed in the United States of America

Contents

Foreword
by Herb Richardson — vii

Introduction: Interview with Carl F.H. Henry
by Kendig Brubaker Cully — 1

Evangelical Identity
by James Wallis and Wes Michaelson — 7

The Battle for the Bible
by Donald T. Williams, Tim Erdel and Tom Garber — 23

The House Divided
by Stephen Board — 31

Our Planet's in Peril
by William F. Willoughby — 37

Christian-Secular Battle Lines
by David Virtue — 43

Faith, Science Can Co-Exist
by William F. Willoughby — 49

Why Christians Differ Politically — 53

Morals and Politics
by David E. Kucharsky — 61

Making of a Christian Mind
by Stephen Board — 73

Concerns and Considerations
by Kenneth Kantzer — 81

Evangelicals' Influence Continues Its Upsurge — 93

Humanism, Christianity Will Clash — 99

Christians in Politics — 105

Worldview of a Theologian — 115

Easter: Decisive for the Christian Faith
by William F. Willoughby — 125

Wheaton and the Evangelicals
by Paul Woo — 131

Shall We Fear God? — 137

The Resurrection Is What Life Is All About
by William F. Willoughby — 143

Devout Theologian
    by James R. Newby and Elizabeth S. Newby   149
Why We Need Christian Think Tanks
    by Beth Spring   159
Talking with Carl Henry
    by Wendy Lee Sereda   165
Christianity and Government
    by Edward Rowe and David Juroe   175
Where the Church Stands   185

Foreword

Dr. Carl Henry's special contribution, for many years, has been to provide intellectual leadership to the evangelical tradition. His work has comprised not merely the writing of several volumes of theology and ethics, but also analyzing and responding to the particular issues of our time. Since the American frontier is not merely a geographical, but also a spiritual place, we should see Dr. Henry as one of the most important Christian Frontiersmen of our time.

Dr. Henry is not merely a theologian. Early on he recognized the importance of the media for shaping our understanding of today's issues and, even more importantly, directing our responses. Therefore, he chose journalism as a second sphere of his vocational activity. As Founding Editor of *Christianity Today*, Carl Henry created an influential and penetrating forum for the discussion of intellectual and social issues from the evangelical viewpoint. And though he has moved on from that editorial work to the authoring of several major books in theology and ethics, we see — in the interviews in this volume — that he retains that ability of a well-trained journalist to focus, clarify, and unforgettably express the point of difficult issues.

When we read a book written by an author, that author is usually hidden from us. In the book we find only his ideas, his thoughts. But when we read an *interview* with an author, then that author is fully present before us. He is there to be questioned, to respond, to clarify, and even to object. The interview format has, therefore, the unique advantage of making us personally acquainted with someone. In any interview, we experience someone there and talking; so after reading these interviews, every one of us will better know —and better admire — Carl Henry, himself.

From another perspective, this volume is also a testimony to the amazing quantity and quality of religious journalism in our time. We should not forget that in every one of these interviews, there is an *interviewer*. Among them are William Willoughby, Louis Cassels, Kendig Brubaker Cully and others who are among the best of our time. These religious journalists, and the remarkable range of publications which they represent, constitute an amazing institutional achievement. It is their questions, their transcriptions, and their edited copy that bring to us Dr. Henry in all the fullness of his words and personal presence. Theirs is an important public art. Yet here, let us pause and remember that Carl Henry is also one of *them*. In fact, *primus inter pares*.

In the two vocations — theologian and journalist — which Carl Henry has so giftedly moulded into one, we have an evangelical Christian Frontiersman who moves ahead and clears the trail for us to follow. In these interviews, Henry shows himself for what he is: intellectually evangelical, passionate yet charitable, wide-ranging, sensible, and true.

Herbert Richardson
Toronto

Introduction:
Interview with Carl F.H. Henry

WHILE THE EDITORS were in Palo Alto, California for a family wedding, a local paper reported that Carl F.H. Henry was in town speaking on the Stanford University campus. Some telephone inquiries to the offices of the university chaplain and the united campus ministry failed to yield clues as to precisely where he was holding forth, but eventually the office of Peninsula Bible Church gave details. He was speaking in the geology corner of the main quad under the auspices of World Vision International, for which he is a staff lecturer, but no one seemed to know where he was staying.

The adventure of trying to find the geology corner on a dark night when the campus was mostly deserted is a thing in itself. Suffice it to say that K.B.C. found his way there, in order to seek an interview with Dr. Henry. I found the corner, and the man, but his lecture was over, though I did get in on another speaker's lengthy speech and some of Henry's answers to questions. It was worth the effort, as it turned out, for we were able to agree to meet at his motel the next morning for a leisurely conversation. Just in time, for he was about to leave for Asia.

Henry might be described as belonging to the evangelical jet set. He is internationally recognized as one of the principal leaders of the evangelical movement, and certainly one of its chief intellectuals. His books include *The Uneasy Conscience of Modern Fundamentalism* and *Christian Personal Ethics*. He was founding editor of *Christianity Today* and served in that post for 12 years. He chaired a world congress on evangelism at Berlin in 1966 and was program chairman for the Jerusalem congress on biblical prophecy in 1970. He has been a professor of theology at Northern Baptist and Fuller Theological Seminaries.

2   Conversations with Carl Henry

We began talking about his current literary labors in theology. Publishers have been prodding him, he said, to write a book with a title such as *Confessions of a Nonconformist*. But "I want to do serious theology rather than personal reflections first. I'm at work on a four-volume set, and have turned over to a publisher the first volume, on God, revelation, and authority. The canopy volume for the first three volumes will be entitled *God Who Speaks and Shows*, which will be on enscripturated and incarnational revelation. The final volume will be on the nature of God. I project as the title for that, *God Who Stands, Stoops, and Stays*—governance, providence, and eschatology."

Does this mean that Henry thinks it still possible to produce a total dogmatic? "I square off with the anti-intellectualist tradition in modern theology, which I think has been a great tragedy." Does he have some things in common with Karl Barth, then? "Not in common at that particular point. I do have in common with Barth his emphasis on the specially revealed God, God known in his revelation, and the rejection of any attempt to get to the living God from a non-god. But to define that self-disclosure non-cognitively, and to exclude general or universal revelation from his disclosure, as Barth did, seems to me to forego a great deal of the heritage."

But is there a similarity between Barth's grand architectonic and the series Henry is projecting? "Much more modest, because I won't get to separate volumes on christology or anthropology any more. Once I had these ambitions. I did a major *Christian Personal Ethics* that's probably in 50,000 libraries today, and Oxford would have published it except that they felt they would have had to put too big a sales price on it. Wilbur Ruggles told me that they'd publish it—two of the three readers had recommended publication—but I'd have to cut it down to three-fifths of its size. So I gave it to Eerdmans. I wanted to do *Christian Social Ethics* alongside that, but the years at *Christianity Today* simply precluded that, and I haven't had secretarial help. So my production has been limited. But it will be—it is—a reasoned effort. In a sense Barth disparaged all prolegomenon to theology, all apologetics. My first volume is on prolegomenon, which is back to the tradition in theology. I'll give Vol. 1 to introduc-

Introduction: Interview with Carl F.H. Henry 3

tory principles and apologetic concerns, wrestling objections to the Christian point of view, and trying to show that they are not really logical. Vols. 2 and 3 will be, then, an exposition of divine revelation in 15 principles that are a sort of rubric for me."

Who are the audience today for this kind of formal theology? "There is no question about the fact that we have in the modern scene an anti-intellectual mood. If you read the lists of annual reading that come out in *The New York Times* and other publications, serious theologians and philosophers are seldom represented any more. This is not so much due to the pragmatic, anti-intellectualist, and sensate orientation of the masses as to the prevalent mood among theologians and philosophers themselves, who have unwittingly invited and accommodated this sort of mood. Most modern theology and philosophy has as little permanently therapeutic significance or value as a massage parlor." (That phrase about the "massage parlor" was apparently a current one with Henry, for he was quoted in the Palo Alto newspaper as having said the same thing in an address the preceding month in Washington, though there, according to the quotation, he referred only to theology, not mentioning philosophy.)

He continued: "The infatuation with novelty in theology finally has a way of wearing itself out. I think that what we need to do is to address the mood beyond this. As I see the intellectual tradition in the 19th and 20th centuries, it seems to me that many scholars have progressively divested themselves of the garments of the Christian heritage, and have now got to the point where they are intellectual nomads who are at the very threshold of final revolt against the heritage. Having practically undressed themselves of the tradition, they are tiring of looking at their own navels. The existentialists are now either forced to try to get out of their own skins in terms of ultimate despair, or they are going to have to be forced back to a recanvassing of the heritage." He interpreted the heritage in terms of what he called "a scripturally controlled message," rather than any "compromise" of it "in the medieval period or ever since."

Does Henry see a new apologetic concern among evangelicals which takes the total cultural contest into consideration more than in an earlier period? "Yes, I think this is so. I think I've had a modest part in nudging the evangelical movement toward a concern for Christian social ethics as well as personal ethics. I think the young evangelicals are reaching out even more vigorously beyond 'Uneasy Conscience' to deliberate participation and engagement in the sociocultural scene. I think that *Christianity Today* more recently has failed to give the guidance for that sort of penetration, and has had more of an observer role than it needed to have had in terms of intellectual leadership at this frontier. The young evangelicals tend to move with far less precision and tend to be vulnerable to some of the mistakes of the past."

In response to a question as to whether he thinks serious theological work has come out of the so-called "neo-evangelical" movement, he outlined three developmental steps: (1) "the correlation under the umbrella of *Christianity Today* of qualified evangelical scholars in all major denominations as well as in the interdenominational movement"; (2) "the production of the evangelical symposia, which were the corporate effort of scholars—that whole 'Contemporary Evangelical Thought' series, volumes of which were published by Harper, Harcourt Brace and others"; (3) "the production of serious theology. It's one of the great tragedies, I think, that you find seminary professors producing potboilers that reach out to the masses; also, many of them feel that this is not the time for serious theology (from my point of view it is always the time for it). What is desperately needed is a modern Augustine who can speak to the whole field. In the last analysis the anti-intellectual drift today can lead in only one direction—to a revival of pre-Christian melancholia. Only the Christian message can offer any cohesive and integrative, logical hope for contemporary mankind."

Other subjects entered our conversation. How about dialogue with Roman Catholic theologians? ("There's as much diversity in Roman Catholic theology today as there is in Protestant theology. The most significant development in Roman Catholic theology is the biblical movement in the 20th century.") Does he see any affinity between the 1st and the emerging 21st centuries? "Yes, very much so. The church is again a conspicuous minority battling all the revived moral operations of paganism."

Whom among his contemporaries does Henry find interesting? ("The most influential theologians have each recaptured some isolated strand of biblical theology and have tried to mount an influential ingress into the contemporary ideological confusion by an exaggerated emphasis on that one isolated segment or strand. Every contemporary theologian tries to get his jumbo jet aloft on one motor that is revved up to full capacity, only to see it unable to remain airborne and to plummet once again to earth.") Thus: Barth, God's special revelation; Cullmann, saving history; Pannenberg, revelation in universal history; Bultmann, authentic human being. "The power of modern theology derives from its borrowed remnants of biblical theology; the vulnerability of contemporary theology derives from the neglect of other aspects without which the force of these isolated elements is soon spent."

Carl Henry's well-trained mind, his worldwide contacts, and his position of eminence among evangelical scholars will all combine to keep the theological readership of America on the alert for his forthcoming four-volume summation. (*The Review of Books and Religion*, mid-February, 1976.)

Sojourners' editor Jim Wallis and associate editor Wes Michaelson interview theologian Carl F.H. Henry. Dr. Henry is internationally recognized as one of the principal leaders of the evangelical movement. He was the founding editor of *Christianity Today*, has been a professor of theology at Northern Baptist and Fuller Theological Seminaries, and is the author of countless books and articles. He is currently writing a monthly series in *Christianity Today* entitled "Evangelicals in Search of Identity."

Evangelical Identity

Q. What are some of the key issues involved in an evangelical identity now, in terms of direction, and especially in relationship to the young evangelical phenomenon?
Dr. Henry. We're at a time when loose coalitions of special evangelical emphases have been emerging. I think the young evangelicals especially represent that sort of loose coalition of particular concerns. While it's good that we begin to understand each other, I don't think that one will ever get from this sort of cross-pollination what the evangelical movement ideally ought to be.

What is missing is, first of all, a vision for the comprehensive truth of God. You get the left shooting at the right, the right shooting at the left; the four spiritual laws emphasis and the social gospel emphasis lining up against each other; and the inerrancy group lining up against those who compromise inerrancy. So the potential for division seems to overhang the modern situation as fully as the encouraging signs of conversation and liaison.

Secondly, there is the lack of a sense of body in the evangelical community. It is fragmented. Some people call it American independency, which permeates the evangelical community. But it's more than that. There's an excessive spirit of independence that characterizes evangelicals almost world wide.
Q. What would a comprehensive view of God's revelation begin to look like?
A. It would involve, certainly, the priority of the truth God declares. If revelation isn't intelligible, we're at a loss to say anything about God and his purposes for man. Secondly, it must include the righteousness that God demands, both public and private righteousness, personal holiness and social justice. Thirdly, the grace God offers, the evangel, would be included.
Q. Do you feel that this comprehensive view, to give identity and unity to evangelicals, would only be around the under-

standing of scriptural inerrancy which is laid out by the Evangelical Theological Society?

A. I would say that the biblical emphasis falls first and foremost on the authority of Scripture. After that, the emphasis falls, it seems to me, on the inspiration of God's word. It is what God has spoken; that's why it is authoritative. The notion of an authoritative word that isn't God's word, or that isn't inspired, is out of view.

Inerrancy seems to me to be an inference from the inspiration that the Bible teaches. If one denies inerrancy, and affirms errancy, he raises all sorts of questions about inspiration. The affirmation of the errancy of Scripture introduces a principle of instability into the authority of Scripture that leads to a lack of agreement as to what parts of Scripture are to be considered authoritive and what parts are not.

Q. In seeking to clarify the meaning of evangelicalism, are you defining evangelicals on the basis of a particular view of inerrancy?

A. Evangelicals are to be known in the world as the bearers of good news in message and life—the good news that God offers new life on the ground of Christ's death and resurrection in the context of a biblically controlled message. That's the emphasis that is characteristically apostolic. Now, the apostles did not go out into the world preaching first and foremost scriptural inerrancy, or a premillenial kingdom, or some of the other things that are made the forefront issues today. These issues are of concern to the Christian community, but they are hardly the umbrella under which one goes out into the world.

Q. It seems that a biblical peoplehood is coming together from a number of traditions and places, one of them being evangelical, but not the only one. And it's a faith that is defined more by a life that is rooted in the Word and is growing out of Scripture than around a precise formulation of a doctrine of Scripture. That's not to say that questions about the nature of Scripture and how we understand it are no longer important. However, perhaps the greatest test of one's biblical fidelity is whether one's life is rooted in the Word, rather than the preciseness of one's doctrinal formulations. Often those that talk about inerrancy are never doing the Word. They are describing the Word, analyzing it, but somehow not doing the

Word. And this goes back to the whole Hebrew notion of what truth is. Can truth be something that we describe and converse about apart from its becoming a part of our lives?

A. Lifestyle is now a growing concern everywhere. In the Bible it has always been a concern. The truth is something that is to be done, not something that is merely to be known. And Christianity rejoices in the one life on earth in which a perfect lifestyle was achieved.

On the other hand, one cannot derive the content of Christian truth from an examination of lifestyle. One could hardly derive even the so-called apostolic kerygma from apostolic life in the world, staggeringly different as Christian life was. How could you ever discern from the apostolic lifestyle the incarnation, or the resurrection of the crucified Lord?

Q. I sometimes wonder if we can even hope for a unified understanding of righteousness, in the personal and public sense you mentioned. Some basic differences within evangelicalism have been rather pronounced for a number of years. It has been argued, by Dayton and others, that there is a discontinuity between the evangelicalism of the nineteenth century and the dominant evangelicalism of the twentieth century. The divisions in the present situation go right back to those old days in the last century where the Princeton school of theology took clear stands against the abolitionist activities of the revivalist evangelicals. On questions of race, women, and economics, the Princeton school was on the side of the status quo, so much so that Hodge's writings were used by pro-slavery apologists in the South to support slavery. Evangelicalism, as Dayton points out, is now dominated by those who root themselves in the line that runs through the Princeton school. Some of us find ourselves increasingly going in different directions and find more resonance with the evangelicalism of the nineteenth century. I wonder if what we mean by public righteousness or the proper relationship of the church to society and state is something that there is going to be real agreement about, given this historical perspective.

A. Let me spell out a position. The Old Testament prophets proclaim universal justice and peace as a prospect assured by the coming Messiah. Christ applies to himself the Old Testament promises and in him the kingdom of God dawns. In the life, death and resurrection of Jesus the victory is already won over all the forces of evil and oppression in the world.

Secondly, Jesus extends that victory in the world in and through the church, the new society of regenerate men and women over which he reigns as head. He extends it by the conquest of Satan and sin in the lives of believers and by the mission that is given to the church in relationship to the world. He extends his victory as well through civil government as a divinely established institution for the promotion of justice which God defines and the restraint of disorder. Part of the obedience which is expected of Christians is their function in relationship to civil government.

The Christian community, in its task of light and salt in the world, is to illumine and salt the world. It has a preservative function, and it fulfills this function in several ways. First, the evangelistic mission which involves a distinctive lifestyle; secondly, the use of one's gifts in the vocational arena to the glory of God and service to his fellow man; and thirdly, the fulfillment of responsibilities in the public arena to civil government. That's the framework within which I work for the extension of the righteousness of Christ in society.

Q. Let me ask two things about that. First, if the church is to be the new society over which Jesus reigns as head, how can those within that new society live their lives in contradiction to Christ's own teaching about the questions of violence and wealth, for instance?

The issue is how we view Christ: whether Jesus Christ is axiomatic for us on a personal, political, and economic level. My basic discomfort with the social ethics of mainline Christendom, be they evangelical or liberal (which to me are usually much closer than most realize) is the failure to come to terms with the incarnation of God in Christ. Jesus Christ, as I understand the New Testament, is not only the means of my atonement, but the pattern for my life. Is Jesus Christ politically axiomatic for the believing community? And if not, then in what sense is the new society a new society?

A. The new society is a society that is transracial, transcultural, transnational, and in which love ideally reigns in all interpersonal relationships. It is a society that is ruled by

Evangelical Identity   11

love. It exists at the same time in relationship to the larger world.

While I agree with you wholly that Jesus is the example of incarnate sonship, I don't think you can infer merely from the lifestyle of Jesus all the criteria that should govern Christian living in the world. Jesus himself gave a teaching role to his disciples and apostles. He wrote nothing and entrusted to the disciples and apostles the role of writing what the Spirit would bring to their remembrance in interpreting his mission. In point of fact, most of the epistles are older than the gospels, and Romans 13 is older than most of the gospels. And while Jesus is in his earthly life the pattern for the believer in the unqualified obedience which he demonstrates to his Father's will and in the fullness of the Holy Spirit in his life, that does not in itself answer the question whether there are aspects to the humiliation of Jesus that attached only to his life in view of his specific redemptive mission—for example, the giving of his life as an atonement without any resistance or countermove toward the powers that crucified him. We stand in an interim period between Jesus' submission to the injustice of Pilate and his return as King of Kings and Lord of Lords when every knee and all the rulers will bow—an interim period in which the New Testament ethic evolves with its legitimate role for the state as an instrument for active promotion of justice and restraint of injustice by the use of force.

Wes, I read your question in the last editorial, "Is it conceivable that a faithful follower of Jesus would push the nuclear button if he were in the White House?" My question is, is it conceivable that Jesus should be walking along the street when some violent aggressor should attack an elderly widow and rape her and not use what force he had to interrupt that, and that he should simply stand by and encourage them to be at peace? Is it conceivable that any act by any person could have such elements of violence and destruction, including Hitler's destruction of six million Jews, that God's response to it would be one other than love?

Q. You say that there are aspects of Christ's humiliation that may be tied to his specifically redemptive mission, and that we then have to look to the corpus of other New Testament teachings. Yet you look to the corpus of New Testament teaching and find continual admonitions to live as Christ lived, to live in Christ, to follow his own pattern, and specific teachings on the very question we have been discussing, never to return evil with evil, to love one's enemies, never to pay back an evil turn with a like gesture, to leave vengeance to God, which is in fact the context of the teaching of Romans 13.

I get uncomfortable when I hear a theologian like yourself, who is continually centering in what God has said, to begin to base an ethic on what one should do when an elderly woman is attacked, or what one does because of who Hitler is. I agree that an ethic needs to be applied to those situations, but it seems dangerous to me to formulate an ethic out of examples or out of the cases and circumstances, rather than beginning with the revelation of God in Jesus Christ. Also, you are dealing in both cases with things that are very emotionally charged.

In a discussion of those issues I would always like to keep coming back to the question of who Jesus Christ is and what that means for us. Then our ethic grows out of the incarnation and of Scripture to the specific instances and the cases in which it must be applied. To say that any reasonable man would have to respond to Hitler in this way is much like the feminist argument you dislike—any reasonable person would have to feel this way, so Paul must be mistaken.

A. The examples that I have are not radically extreme cases. One is an actual turning point in western history and the other is one you can find in the *Washington Post* or *Star* every week. To come back to the example of Jesus, one would need to settle the question of war through an experience in which he or his disciples were involved and in which he gave explicit teaching on the subject. As I see it, no passage drawn from the sermon on the mount explicitly deals with the subject of war. And apart from that, any effort to settle the question of involvement in war is highly inferential. More than inference is involved in the Romans 13 passage.

Q. The legitimacy of civil government is not denied, nor that civil government is used in the providence of God, nor that God's action in history is not limited to the church. God's hand can be in revolution and in war, using that cycle of violence against itself. The question here, though, is the rela-

Evangelical Identity 13

tionship of the Christian to civil government and what part the church of Jesus Christ plays in God's action in history.

A. Very true. But there is a fundamental danger in looking at civil government somewhat deistically, or almost dualistically, as in some of the recent writings in which it is viewed only in the context of demonic powers, rather than as a divinely purposed order of preservation that is as firmly rooted in the will of God, and hence in the intention of Christ, as is the church, at this particular point in history. Civil government has in the purpose of God for history, this side of the end time, a purpose as a divinely structured order of preservation in fallen society as undeniable as his purpose for the church.

Q. Do you think that God's action in bringing about the continuing dawn of the kingdom first demonstrated in the life of His Son is achieved as much through the state as through the church?

A. No.

Q. Do you draw a distinction between the role of the government in restraining disorder, and the role of the government in instituting the new society?

A. Only what is regenerate belongs to the kingdom of God. And the state doesn't regenerate—it preserves ideally in God's name the structures and content of justice.

Q. But in that preservative function, do you feel the Christian has a loyalty to that function on the same level as his loyalty to the church?

A. Whatever loyalties he has, whether to the church or civil government, are loyalties unto God through Christ. Paul doesn't depart from the apostolic principle that where the state demands what God disapproves, the Christian is to obey God rather than man, and that where the state disallows what God requires the Christian ought to disobey the state.

Q. Yes, but I infer that you said the purposes of God's will are just as much for the state, for divinely structured order, as they are for the church.

A. For the state as an instrumentality for certain purposes in a fallen society, yes.

Q. Here I think we are touching one of the issues that is at stake in different strands of evangelicals and where we are going. The kind of reformed theological thinking on these matters, at least for me, gives much too positive a role to the state. It doesn't take seriously enough the fallenness of the state or the state's identity as one of the principalities that the New Testament says are in open rebellion against the purposes of God. Though I would see a providential care of God through the state, the state is never intended to be an instrumentality for bringing in the new order.

A. I agree that the definition of justice and spiritual regeneration are not the government's business.

Q. What concerns me is how this has worked out historically. What has happened in the doing of mainstream social ethics is that the ethics no longer derive from God in Christ but derive from the state or from notions of civil government. Reinhold Niebuhr, for instance, says that the nonresistant, nonviolent Jesus, while most faithful to the historical Christ, is just not adequate for determining public ethics and that we need to derive those ethics for our action in the public, political, and social area from other norms. I can understand how Reinhold Neibuhr does that because of his weak Christology, but I'm alarmed when his is the major text at evangelical colleges teaching political science. A discussion about the New Testament role of the state is in order. But the norms that we take as axiomatic to that discussion must derive from God in Christ and not from the state. Is Jesus the norm for us, or isn't he?

A. There are biblical principles but no comprehensive political philosophy in the New Testament. We have a great deal more about the church as the new society and the way the church is to live her life and govern herself than we do about the church in relationship to the world. We have to remember that the political arena is a vastly changing one, in different places and times.

The church needs to channel informed Christians into the realm of vocation, in law, jurisprudence, political service. And yet the WCC Geneva Conference on Church and Society wholly bipassed Secretary of State Rusk, an active churchman. No effort was made to involve him. Why not along with those who opposed Vietnam involvement? I'm not saying this on behalf of Vietnam now, because I myself at *Christianity Today* assumed the trustworthiness and the nondeceptiveness of some of the statements we were getting from our leaders about Vietnam.

Today we have gone to the opposite extreme in not trusting anything they say. We're on the other binge. But at least it's been a very sobering experience and we no longer take their statements at face value. But it's very difficult to superimpose the post-Watergate, the post-Vietnam situation back upon the years that we were going through then. I myself said in those years, even while I was still editor, that if we did not intend to do what was necessary to bring that war to a conclusion we ought not to be in there at all.

Q. The strategy of infiltrating the systems of the world by Christians through vocation doesn't strike me as a new strategy but as the one being practiced right now. There are Christians in every single vocational area. It seems, though, that those institutions are changing and shaping the Christians in them more than the Christians are changing the institutions.

A. The church has not itself effectively taught scriptural principles to her own sons, who have gone on into these various spheres of vocations. This is the great tragedy. When I was a young fellow your age, many of the Christians in the agencies in Washington were the sons of social gospel ministers, those sons who had become disenchanted with the concept of ministry and went in with a social gospel philosophy. The church needs to become a center in which the biblical social ethic is learned no less than the personal ethic.

Q. My experience is that when you get involved in the political order, you then are asked continually to compromise, relegate, reinterpret, or dismiss central New Testament teachings in order to preserve your own place within the order, or to preserve the government itself on the terms which it defines. To gain power within the system, I have to play according to its rules which are part of a fallen order, directly in contradiction to the kingdom that I have given my life to.

A. There is nothing about the order itself as God ordains it that requires it per se to box you in. It is the misuse of what the order is intended to be, by compromised people and groups. Involvement in it, in the context which you suggest, gives a Christian a perfect platform out of which to interpret what the order is doing, how it is cutting across Christian concerns, and to speak a Christian witness to it precisely in that situation.

Without minimizing all that you have said, even in these

circumstances it seems to me that we must not totally withdraw. We must rather use the situation as fully as possible. Little as has been achieved, it is nevertheless worthwhile. The Christian can count upon the providence of God to take our meager efforts even in a compromised situation, and even if we ourselves don't act infallibly in this arena, the providence of God can preserve and multiply our efforts in the political sphere.

I think Joseph in Egypt had his role and he still has his role in modern times. At the right moment the right opportunity comes, when people either turn to the Christian out of frustration, or when he finds an appropriate opportunity to exercise his influence, whether he does it through re-election or whether he does it like Brooks Hays, who if he had waited four years and compromised on the race issue would have been elected, but who in good conscience refused to compromise and lost.

Q. Even Joseph's position came by way of prison.
A. Yes.
Q. But that's a crucial point. There's a difference in one's being used of God in God's timing, out of a believing community of people where one's identity and one's norms for life and action derive. Then God can use the community or the person in the secular order. What's important to me is our own faithfulness, and if God in the course of history chooses to use that for a larger purpose, well, praise God. And if not, still praise God. I don't see anywhere in Scripture the instruction to gain power for influencing institutions in the world that social action people talk so much about.

The crucial question here for me is not participation in or outside of the system, but on what terms are we active and involved? Most of the thinking and activity that has gone on under the banner of Christian political and social involvement, both ecumenical and evangelical, is much more on the world's terms than on the terms of the kingdom. To act on the terms of the kingdom is not the same as withdrawal. Christians now and down through history, out of an allegiance to Christ's kingdom, have been decisively involved in ways that are peripheral to the established ways of involvement yet historically wind up being those most decisive in terms of the shape of history.

A. A great deal that passes for Christian social ethics today overlooks the primary responsibility for Christians to care for those within the body, simply because we have little sense of body within Christian circles any longer.

I see a regrouping of evangelical forces for power and realignment. And it's not only on the right wing; it's also on the left. What we need is a deep realization of our emptiness, even if we should succeed in our smaller visions of what is needed. The world is in such tragic shambles today. It's a pit of anguish.

Yet when you look at the evangelical community, what do you hear them say? In one whole wing, four spiritual laws. In another whole wing, radical social activism. Where is the sense of the *new community*? I'm convinced that it isn't going to come by an organizational evangelical ecumenicity emerging into some giant framework of the existing evangelical agencies. They can find ways of understanding and cooperating, but that isn't the way the new family is going to come into being. Do we have to wait for the dropping of an atom bomb or for some national calamity?

It can come only through repentance and prayer and reawakening. It will have to come out of a great sense of emptiness and longing, a transcendent initiative that crowns a sense of emptiness and hunger on the part of God's people. I don't sense a depth of hunger and yearning that really seems to answer to the anguish of the world in our time.

Q. The rebuilding of the church is to me the most important thing that we need to be about. That sense comes out of a number of things. One is a very radical understanding of the kingdom as a new order. Secondly, the common life of that new community is the key to understanding God's action in history. Community is not a substitution for involvement, but the means of our engagement with the world. Out of that, there needs to be a daily involvement with the poor, understanding that the Christian community is to look at the systems of the world through the eyes of the victims of those systems and to make community with the poor, which is different from being an ecclesiastical lobby on behalf of the poor from a position of comfort and power. Out of that base there needs to be visible protest and confrontation with the forces of death and the pursuing of alternatives. On those four counts I am increasingly depressed about the evangelical establishment.

A. Let me ask about this, because World Vision has a deep commitment to the poor, as you know. Don't you feel that, number one, if we don't lick the problem of inflation the whole world may be in trouble in another generation? Number two, don't you think that the problem of providing jobs is one critically important facet of attack on the poverty problem?

Q. But don't you think that then inevitably raises the questions of what are the systemic causes of that unemployment and of that poverty?

A. Yes, the raising of this issue inevitably raises the question of structural changes. The Christian community can't avoid the obligation to raise questions of unjust structures. On the one hand, I don't share the view that demeans what the Christian does into simply a bandaid or aspirin dispenser operation because I am grateful for the type of humanitarianism that Christianity released in its history. But I wholly agree that it's not the place to stop, and the question of just structures is one that must be raised in the economic as well as in other arenas.

I think there are strengths to capitalism. But our failure to criticize capitalism in its operation—the shoddy record of production for obsolescence, the reckless depletion of natural resources, the prizing of profit over sensitivity to workers' needs, the bribery by multinational corporations, the big stake in smoking and cigarette production, despite the fact that we know it to be harmful, the alcohol traffic—gave a one way street to the Marxists to criticize capitalism, in such a way that our younger generation became enchanted with Marxism as an alternative.

Q. In terms of questions related to the structures of power, why is it that almost across the board, the structures of evangelicalism are time after time—by association, by relationship, or by outright conviction—on the side of the rich, not the poor, the white, not the non-white, of the powerful and not the powerless?

Is the kind of mainline evangelicalism that goes through the Princeton school right back to the Reformation, is that theology inherently supportive of the status quo or at best a mild sort of reformism? Is there something inherent in that

theology that is socially and politically resistant to change?
A. What happened in part was this. People came into the evangelical churches who had little and became successful because of the new virtues, the new drives, and the new integrity. All of this contributed to their success, and these resources grew up within the churches and became available to support enterprises. It's impossible to launch a movement without financial support.

When we launched *Christianity Today* a lot of people thought that J. Howard Pew was the benefactor. Pew was a large donor but we could have never survived with simply the gifts that Pew gave us. We had Northern Republicans. We had Southern Democrats. I didn't know what some of their politics were. So *Christianity Today* in its support had a considerable diversity.

Now, in regard to becoming poor, the Christian is called in the New Testament to show compassion for those in need and to use what he has as a divine stewardship. I don't see any necessity in the New Testament for any personal redistribution of all one's properties as long as he has a lifestyle that honors God and uses what he has as a stewardship.

A community of goods was practiced voluntarily by the Jerusalem church, but there is no necessity for this to be universally imposed upon believers. I think we need to rethink the matter of lifestyle; however, I don't think the Christian community can bear the massive burden of poverty in the world.

Q. The conclusion seems to be coming from economic studies that western civilization cannot continue to live in the way in which we now do if there is to be a true sense of compassion for all humanity.

A. Unless one could come up with data, argued data, to show that sheer redistribution would not within a remarkably short time simply deteriorate again into a repetition of the same circumstances, I think that Christians are far better off to avoid legalistic solutions and to probe possibilities that are job producing—to try to set up industries and this sort of thing. That represents a far sounder use of funds than simply an automatic leveling.

What needs to be shown, and I doubt that it can be, is that

if I eat less hamburger or that if I eat less beef, it will provide more grain or more food for the person out in Africa.

Q. It won't necessarily. But what is true is that if everyone continues to eat the same amount of grain through beef consumption, for instance, the resource base of protein grain for all humanity will continue to be monopolized. I think it does raise the question of how much our lives as Christians are tied into the present economic order and how much is that present economic order sustained ultimately at the expense of the world's poor.

A. Yes, and the correlation of what is done in the West with nations that do the most that they can to solve their own problems, in contrast with nations that through lack of population control simply extend the problem.

Q. I would like to get back to the third thing you mentioned earlier—the gospel that God offers. Are there inherent things in particular formulations of evangelical theology that are resistant to fundamental change in the social order?

For example, what the gospel means is itself still a very controversial question. What is the evangel?

The traditional view would say that the heart of the gospel is justification by faith, the atonement, getting one's heart right with God. Then there are social implications and political responsibilities that derive from that. Others would say that the meaning of Jesus is the inauguration of a new order of things. Whenever you delete the coming and the meaning of the kingdom from the proclamation of the gospel, the inseparable unity between justification by faith and participation in the kingdom of God is broken. Reconciliation is required because to participate in that new order requires a change so fundamental that the apostle calls it a new birth.

In the nineteenth century evangelism that resulted in so much social initiative, the meaning of the kingdom was kept in a central place. Now the kingdom imperative is on the periphery and neglected or removed altogether so that what you have is a gospel defined by the four spiritual laws. That theology seems to me to be inherently susceptible to being used to sanction the social order the way it is.

A. The twentieth century evangelical movement found itself in a religious context that was not characteristic of the nineteenth century movements. It was the context of an ecclesiastical power which spoke for Christianity in the larger world community, deleted the importance of personal regeneration, and conceived the evangel essentially in terms of socio-political change. Hence the evangelical movement promoted its evangel in a reactionary way, centering the evangel in personal regeneration and deploring socio-political activity as a mere extra-curricular activity.

In the two definitions of the evangel that you give, I think the second is the authentic one. Though the evangel is the proclamation of the coming of the new order, it must be no less central than the first. The substitutionary death and resurrection of Christ as the ground of God's gift of the forgiveness of sins and new life in Christ reaches far beyond inner-personal concerns to the whole of interhuman relationships. The good news is that the righteous God of history has won victory over the forces of evil and the powers that would do us to death. On the ground of Jesus' death and resurrection we are offered the forgiveness of sins, new life, and a place in God's kingdom. We belong to the new society, which Christ rules as risen head, that will pass over into eternity. This society is indignant of unrighteousness wherever it exists in personal and social relationships. It shares with Christ the longing for the coming in its fullness of the new heavens and earth where righteousness prevails throughout of the whole of it. And, no one can really stand on New Testament terrain unless he tries to be as explicit about the justice God demands as about the justification that God offers. That's the big task for us in this turning time in human civilization.

Dr. Harold Lindsell's new book, *The Battle for the Bible* (Zondervan, 1976), has cast down the theological gauntlet against evangelical defectors from the doctrine of biblical inerrancy. The book has brought to the surface a controversy which has long been building within modern evangelicalism. To help our readers understand the current situation, the *Scribe* is pleased to present an interview with Dr. Carl F.H. Henry, founding editor of *Christianity Today* and currently visiting professor of Systematic Theology at Trinity. Participating were Donald T. William, editor of the *Scribe*; Tim Erdel, editor of the *Trinity Journal*; and Tom Garber, past editor of *Nose and Newts*.

The Battle for the Bible

Q. Why don't we begin with a short statement of your own present position on the doctrine of Scripture, and how this relates to what you have held in the past.
Dr. Henry. My position today is precisely what it has been through the years. I hold unequivocally to the authority, the inspiration, and the inerrancy of Scripture; and I think that any questioning of one or all of those emphases represents a departure from what the Bible teaches, explicitly or implicitly, a departure from the perspective of Jesus Christ and the apostles, and a departure from the historic Christian position.
Q. Then, statements of yours which have appeared recently in periodicals such as *Time Magazine* must be taken in context of that affirmation?
A. Oh yes. There have been a number of statements recently which have been formulated in the context of Harold Lindsell's book *The Battle for the Bible*; and unfortunately, the statement in *Time* implied, because of the way in which it appeared, that somehow I am more sympathetic to the Fuller position than the Lindsellian position. And, of the two, I have far *less* in common with the Fuller position. In fact, I read Dr. Hubbard's convocation response to Lindsell's book, and I thought it was an oblique and really unworthy statement that did not wrestle the issues.

Then, you may ask why I have reservations about Dr. Lindsell's book. What I was quoted in magazines and newspapers as saying about the volume needs to be understood in several contexts: first, the reactions I have as the founding editor of *Christianity Today*; and second, in the broader context of historic evangelical theology. When I said that Dr. Lindsell wages an atom bomb theological warfare that destroys as many evangelical friends as foes, I mean two things. The first concerns *Christianity Today* and its strategy. When the magazine began, it was committed editorially to the doctrine of inerrancy as a test of evangelical *consistency*. We did not hesitate to express that conviction editorially, or to enlist essayists in support of it. But from the beginning we had as key contributing editors evangelicals who did not believe in inerrancy, yet who joined us in bold theological witness on other doctrines to the non-evangelical world. We used all soldiers where they fought well and fought best. At no time during my editorship did we escalate the doctrine of inerrancy into a test of evangelical *authenticity*. And I think that is what the Lindsell volume does. Thus to divide the evangelical community into sheep and goats over the issue of inerrancy seems to me an unfortunate tactic for *Christianity Today*. It will sacrifice the enthusiasm and cooperation of one whole wing of the conservative theological witness today, precisely at a time when we need all the energies we can enlist in the battle. I think it highly unfortunate that the *primary* thing that should now be said about men like F.F. Bruce and Berkouwer, men who have made significant contributions to the conservation position—even though we might have hoped for somewhat more from them—is that they are not authentic evangelicals because of their position at this one point.

Secondly, I think the problem is deeper than merely a difference of strategy. Although at the beginning of his volume Dr. Lindsell says that he does not intend to imply that one who does not believe in inerrancy cannot be a Christian, or belong to the company of the redeemed, nevertheless, before he ends the volume he gives the clear *implication* that those who disown inerrancy are indeed headed for final wrath and doom. For example, on page 211, he clearly seems to say that those who give up inerrancy are the tares among the wheat which the angels will remove at the end of the age. This is an unfortunate and excessive statement; it goes beyond any biblical license.

Beyond that, the volume lacks theological balance. My conviction is that the first thing the Bible says about itself is not its inerrancy or its inspiration, but its authority. That the prophets and the apostles speak the Word of God and therefore speak authoritatively, is in the forefront of the Bible. Just as in the gospels the most important thing is the incarnation, death and resurrection, while the *how* of the incarnation, the virgin birth, lies in the hinterland; so also in respect to the doctrine of Scripture, while inspiration is as clearly taught as the virgin birth, it lies rather in the hinterland. The Bible teaches its authority and inspiration explicitly, while inerrancy, it seems to me, is an inference from this.

Now, Dr. Lindsell takes Warfield's view that inerrancy is clearly taught in Scripture. But at least Warfield gives the passages which he affirms to teach the doctrine; Dr. Lindsell gives none. Also, Warfield did not lodge the whole case for Christian theism on inerrancy, but went on to say that even if the Bible were only as accurate, let us say, as United Press International, we would still be faced with a life and death decision about salvation in Christ. I would say that inerrancy is clearly implied, logically deduced from, and a necessary correlative of inspiration, though not *explicitly* taught. This is not, however, my primary difference with Lindsell. Rather it is his inversion of emphasis through which inerrancy becomes the first and primary issue in the discussion of Scripture.

Q. One of the reasons Dr. Lindsell thinks that inerrancy is so *crucial* is what he tries to document as the *consequences* of giving it up, that it puts you in grave danger of giving up authority as well. Dr. Jewett, who takes it upon himself now to disagree with the apostle Paul, seems to bear this out. If you disagree with Dr. Lindsell's strategy, what suggestions would you have as to how we *do* go about insisting on inerrancy as a mark of evangelical consistency, if not authenticity?

A. I have always insisted that those who reject inerrancy have never adduced any objective principle, either biblical, philosophical, or theological, that enables them to distinguish between those elements which are supposedly errant in Scripture and those which are not. That's what I mean by evangelical consistency. Once inerrancy is abandoned, one is involved in an unstable epistemology, in which one resists further compromise, not by a consistent regard for epistemic principle, but solely by an act of will.

Q. One of the theses for which Dr. Lindsell has been criticized is his "domino theory," that giving up inerrancy does lead necessarily to further declension. Do you yourself know of any institution which has *not* followed through on the domino theory after giving up inerrancy?

A. I think that Lindsell's domino theory is far closer to the truth when applied to institutions rather than to individuals, but I don't think he carefully makes that distinction. This happens in institutions for two reasons. First, administration and faculty in institutions soon learn to manipulate blocks of power in relation to various wings of their supportive constituency. Secondly, faculty members who make compromises plead academic freedom and invoke the spectre of the displeasure of accrediting associations if pressures are brought to bear upon them for their views. Factors are at work which are not so potent in terms of individual experience, although eccumenical agencies often trade power and prominence for tolerance and exert a different sort of pressure.

Q. As one of the founders of the modern evangelical movement, does the present situation in regards to inerrancy cause you great concern about the future of the movement?

A. First, I disown that I *am* one of the founders of the movement, because I don't think its roots are modern, they are biblical. Nor do I think that inerrancy is a recent commitment of the Church, inspired by Hodge and Warfield, as some of the young socially active evangelicals seem to imply. It is implicit in the New Testament, it was the doctrine of the early Church, it was held by Roman Catholicism at least until Vatican II, and the Protestant Reformers are on that side. At the same time, Dr. Lindsell's contention that inerrancy is the special theological concern of our century is not wholly accurate. Even in the late seventeenth century, intellectuals in Europe were having to make a decision at this point, as some of Prof. John Woodbridge's research is bringing out, and all the present issues were part of that debate.

But be that as it may, in the light of current epistemological confusion Dr. Lindsell's book could be the preliminary call for a massive re-alignment of evangelical forces. He specifically calls upon laymen in key positions to bring pressure to bear on institutions for conformity to inerrancy. This, along with the volume's association with *Christianity Today*, its endorsement by Billy Graham, and its forward by Dr. Ockenga, the founder of the N.A.E., makes it more important than just another book. This leads me to some aspects of the book which I think are evangelically divisive.

Dr. Lindsell regards the historical-critical method as in itself an enemy of orthodox Christian faith. He seems totally unaware that even evangelical seminaries of which he approves are committed to historical criticism, while repudiating the arbitrary, destructive presuppositions upon which the liberal use of the method is based. Surely Dr. Lindsell does not want the seminaries to take an uncritical, unhistorical approach to the Bible! So, I'm troubled about the possibilities of a vast amount of misunderstanding among the laity in view of excessive statements, and exaggerated perspectives, that may only encourage some younger scholars to escape the force of Dr. Lindsell's real intentions.

Now, your question was, "How do I feel about the current situation?" I think the current situation is a theological shambles. The ecumenical movement has brought the neoprotestant era into a time of unresolved crisis, particularly in the area of religious knowledge. On any assessment the situation is disturbing. The increasing doctrinal ignorance among laymen, and the defection of many seminaries are matters of great concern.

One of the finest sections in Dr. Lindsell's book is its survey of Fuller Theological Seminary, where the faculty has been unable to keep faith with two successive statements of its view of Scripture. Until recently, after revising the original statement, they held the line at least in respect to faith and morals; but with Dr. Jewett's contention that the apostle Paul erred on the issue of the subordination of women, there is a breaching of the inerrancy of Scripture also at the level of Christian practice, or ethics.

Dr. Lindsell's book says many things that needed to be said. There are issues that need to be faced by the churches. The doctrine of inerrancy is to me not a dispensable doctrine, and the Church has nothing to gain by evading the issue. My disagreements with the book are rather in the areas of context, balance and theological perspicuity.

Yet one gets out of Dr. Lindsell's volume an impression that the evangelicals are now simply a ghetto-operation. What you don't get is the realization that there is a vast tide of sympathy for our view in many spheres. Many of the people who represent our views are lonely individuals, but they have great gifts, and *could* be brought together, at least for an intellectual witness, if not in other ways. Nor does *The Battle for the Bible* give us the sense that the Bible is battling for us, and that the *other* views are in desperate trouble, struggling to escape ever encroaching skepticism by any and every possible means. (*The [Trinity] Scribe*, June 1, 1976.)

The outstanding quality of Carl F.H. Henry's career has been its sense of the *strategic*. Henry is a master strategist for the evangelical viewpoint as well as one of its most constructive critics. For these reasons *Eternity* welcomes Dr. Henry's tightly-packed insights into the problems of evangelical identity and unity.

The House Divided:
"The disciples were discussing among themselves as to who of them was the most evangelical . . ."

Q. Do you regard the widening controversy over "genuine evangelicals" as much ado about nothing?
Dr. Henry. By no means. The question of a true evangel (versus "any other gospel," cf. Gal. 1:9) and of the evangel's undiminished relevance for the whole human predicament are centrally important. Anyone who dismisses debate over evangelical authenticity with a discussion of "how many angels can dance on the point of a needle" needs to be awakened to the issues. But that hardly justifies the disposition of some spokesmen to project an "enemies list" disruptive of the body of evangelical believers.
Q. Who on earth *is* an evangelical in your view?
A. An evangelical, in brief, is one who believes the evangel. The Good News is that the Holy Spirit gives spiritual life to all who repent and receive divine salvation proferred in the incarnate, crucified and risen Redeemer. The Christian message is what the inspired Scriptures teach—no more, no less—and an evangelical is a person whose life is governed by the scriptural revelation of God and his purposes.
Q. How is defining the term "evangelical" a peculiarly present-day problem?
A. The problem has an ever-sharpening modern edge. In Germany, Lutheran churches traditionally used the term *Evangelisch* to distinguish themselves from both Roman Catholic and Reformed (Calvinistic) churches. In Latin America the term became synonymous merely with "Protestant" or non-Catholic churches. In England mediating scholars like F.W. Dillistone spoke of themselves as "liberal evangelicals," although strictly speaking such terms blur the logical distinctions as much as do the notions of a fish-fowl or

a fowl-fish. A theological liberal is non-evangelical. The World Council of Churches promoted an impression of evangelical pluralism by referring both to "conservative evangelicals" and "liberal evangelicals," and some American evangelicals obligingly called themselves "conservative evangelicals." The Blake-Pike proposal for world ecumenism, now all-but-forgotten, envisioned a church "catholic, reformed and evangelical." You can see how flexible and confusing the word becomes.

Q. Hasn't the term been more precise in America?

A. When the National Association of Evangelicals adopted it in 1942 and soon rallied ten million affiliates in its constituency, ecumenical liberals disparaged and demeaned the term. N.A.E. identified with the evangelical awakening in England, the Protestant Reformation and finally with New Testament Christianity. Although denominations like the Evangelical and Reformed Church which reflect an ecumenical identity, or even the Evangelical Covenant Church of America which reflects growing ecumenical influence, blur the term's significance, its primary American intention was to signal historic Christian orthodoxy. The more liberal churchmen found the label desirable only when the evangelical movement became vigorous.

Today religious movements of many kinds borrow the term and seek to use it to their special purposes. They virtually span the alphabet: Anglican evangelicals, Catholic evangelicals, charismatic evangelicals, liberationist evangelicals, pacifist evangelicals, political evangelicals, and so on. Failure of the evangelical colleges, seminaries, magazines and journals to articulate a comprehensive and definitive evangelical theology unwittingly abets this confusion.

Q. Why have evangelicals insisted so strenuously on the authority of the Bible?

A. God has so identified his redemptive revelation with the prophetic-apostolic Scriptures that the loss of scriptural authority clouds salvation itself. The demeaning of biblical authority with the consequent dwarfing of the content of Scripture inevitably warps the Christian system of doctrine.

In one of his earliest epistles the apostle Paul emphasizes, and indeed reiterates, that the Christian fundamentals are biblical controlled: "Christ died for our sins *according to the Scriptures* and was buried and rose again the third day *according to the Scriptures*" (I Cor. 15:3-4).

Many modern commentaries swayed by critical theories seem merely to gloss over this emphasis, proffering some such innocuous comment as that these phrases indicate "an important aspect" of the early Christian message. But the four-letter Greek preposition *Kata* (according to)—*kata* the inspired writings, repeated for inescapable emphasis—declares the Christian Good News (the "evangel") to be scripturally-licensed and authorized. We affirm not humanly originated doctrines but spiritual truths and historical facts long anticipated and foretold by divinely chosen prophets whose authoritative writings were fulfilled in the very lifetime of Paul and his contemporaries.

Q. Would you say regeneration or inerrancy is the prime issue for evangelicals? Which?

A. An unregenerate inerrantist is spiritually worse off than a regenerate errantist. But an unstable view of religious knowledge and authority jeopardizes not only an adequate definition of regeneration but one's insistence on its absolute necessity. The alternatives therefore seem much like choosing whether to have one's right or left leg amputated. The emphasis that "since all one needs to enter heaven is to be 'born again,' why saddle anybody with 'traditions of the evangelical elders'?" falls under its own judgment; one need only read John 3:1-21 to discern that much more than the new birth is indispensable if even its significance is not to be eroded.

Q. Despite commendations by Billy Graham and Harold John Ockenga the reviews of Harold Lindsell's *The Battle for the Bible* (Zondervan, 1976) are less than enthusiastic even in the staunchest evangelical circles. What are your impressions?

A. I have mixed feelings about it, as do many readers. The book contains too much truth to dismiss it merely as polemics and muck-raking. It says some things that need to be said. Yet it turns back the clock some 20 years to when evangelical energies emptied mainly into "telling the truth about *them* (i.e., the opposition)." Because it inadequately states the evangelical alternative many evangelical institutions and publications are refusing to identify themselves with the volume. The all-too-prevalent caricature of evangelicals as unscholarly and uncritical gains credence from its unqualified repudiation of historical critical method (rather than the arbitrary biases to which it is deployed). Likewise such intemperate notions as that those who do not believe in biblical inerrancy are tares to be destroyed in the final judgment. It is not for rejecting inerrancy but for what they have done with the light they have that human beings will be finally judged.

Q. Your hesitation, then, is not so much with the thesis of the book on Scripture, but how it comes across?

A. My disagreements with the book are in the areas of context, balance and theological perspicuity.

Q. Do you think inerrancy is nevertheless worth holding out for?

A. It was Jesus's view, and that of the apostles, and of the church fathers, and of the Roman Catholic Church down to Vatican II. The recent effort to detach the Reformers from that view, and to place them on the side of scriptural errancy, is unpersuasive. It would be high neglect for evangelical Christians in our day, when the inerrancy, inspiration and authority of the Bible are under vigorous attack, to opt out of this discussion. But the task is made more difficult rather than helped when spokesmen correlate inerrancy with the existing translations, with an uncritical approach to the Scriptures, with the branding as false evangelicals of scholars who expound the Bible as reliable though they are noncommital on inerrancy, or the consignment of noninerrantist evangelicals to hell.

We need to preserve biblical balance, and the scriptural emphasis falls, it seems to me, first and foremost on the authority of Scripture, and then on its divine inspiration as the source of that authority; the inerrancy of Scripture is an inference from, and logically implicit in, its divine inspiration. No informed historian will dismiss the emphasis on biblical inerrancy, as do some alienated young evangelicals, as an aberration foisted on the Christian community by the Hodge-Warfield school (Princeton Seminary, 1820-1920).

Q. Why do you think the American evangelical movement has not put its act together?

A. For almost a decade American evangelicals have been in a "holding pattern" except for some momentum in evangelism, growth of conservative churches, and noteworthy gains in divinity student enrolment. No forceful leadership emerged to give incisive direction to dynamic forces concerned for social justice and poltical morality. No significant theological initiative has defined evangelical perspectives powerfully over against contemporary alternatives.

Reactionary criticism turned away young evangelicals while mainstream spokesmen "played it safe"; valuable editorial space in some evangelical publications was given over to trivia. American evangelicals failed to speak powerfully to national conscience, being mainly oriented to a crusade and congregation witness. Meanwhile the gap widened not only between public practice and evangelical morality, but between evangelical *beliefs* and those of worldlings regarding sex, marriage, gambling, shoplifting, work and much else. Yet some evangelical leaders were preening themselves over past achievements, little suspecting that an arrested momentum is the prelude to retrogression and leads on to extreme and radical commitments to compensate for mounting losses.

In the last two weeks I have had unexpected letters from prominent leaders asserting that the unity forged at Lausanne in 1974 is in some circles under heavy strain, that it was a blunder for *Christianity Today* to fracture a long-standing informal international alliance of conservative scholars by their division into true and false evangelicals, that despite the forfeiture of a cooperative Christian university on the American scene the need for it remains so pressing that it should again be considered.

It takes a big heart to shelter such concerns; they do not sit well with a vision diverted inward. In a time of uncertainty the individual empire-builders readily exploit anxieties to entrench their own particular institutions and enterprises. Recent emphases turn the evangelical community's concerns inward upon itself, rather than upward and outward toward an imperiled humanity in need of a sure Word of God in a cause in which the Bible does on-going battle for us all. It is we ourselves who champion God's inerrant Word who will be weighed in the balances for what we have done with it, both internally and externally. (*Eternity*, October 1976).

Dr. Carl F.H. Henry, founding editor of *Christianity Today* magazine, is considered the leading theologian of evangelical Christianity. The author of 23 books, he has just completed the first two volumes of a four-volume work titled *God, Revelation and Authority*, which is receiving praise as the most definitive work on evangelical theology in this century. He was interviewed by *Washington Star* Staff Writer William F. Willoughby.

Our Planet's in Peril

Q. Do you think Christianity is on the skids?
Dr. Henry. It's modern mankind—not the religion of the Bible—that's in dire trouble. The intellectual decision most urgently facing humanity in our time is whether to acknowledge or disown Jesus Christ as the hope of the world and whether Christian values are to be the arbiter of human civilization in the present instead of only in the final judgment of men and nations.
Q. Why are you writing *God, Revelation and Authority*?
A. For three reasons: First, because our generation largely settles for grime when it could reach for glory; it is indifferent to spiritual values. Secondly, because God isn't bullish either on the Communist world or on the free world or on present-day America. Thirdly, because the problem of authority, which haunts all arenas of thought and life today, turns ultimately on the reality of God in his revelation.
Q. How bad do you think things really are?
A. We're living in a civilizational crisis from which no nation on earth is immune because of scientific technology, mass media impact, and political realities; ours is truly a planet in peril.
Q. Doesn't that make you an alarmist?
A. Many scholars who claim to be emotionally detached and to view human events reflectively today voice direful prophecies of impending doom, but mostly for the wrong reasons—overpopulation, famine, depletion of energy, ecological pollution, nuclear destruction, perhaps even astroidal collision. These are not the worst of our woes but they are trouble aplenty. In the department of environmental planning at one major West Coast university, faculty members think that modern culture as we know it has a survival span of only a few centuries. Undergraduate students in the same department see no reason to think that the collapse will not occur before the year 2000 and almost certainly within their own lifetime. That would give us about two decades, perhaps less.

Q. And these are the "wrong reasons" to be worried about?
A. Yes. Even if we find a way around the pressing problems they indicate, the deeper facets of the civilizational crisis remain: the crisis of conscience, the crisis of truth, the crisis of will, the crisis of spirit—in short, the moral and spiritual dilemma that has overtaken our generation; the breakdown of authority; the confusion concerning transcendent reality; the subjectivizing of God; and with all this the loss of the worth and meaning of personal survival.

Q. Are there no answers?
A. Neither empirical science nor secular philosophy can be of decisive help. Observational science offers no finalities. It has to hedge all bets: Revising whatever it says about anything and everything is the price it pays for what we call scientific progress. In any event, science cannot identify God and the good because its method is inappropriate to such realities. Science has made life sometimes more convenient and more comfortable, but it has made us neither wiser nor better—just more knowledgeable about ever-changing phenomena and about techniques that a generation lacking in moral sensitivities can deploy in disregard of ethical principles and values. Science cannot identify fixed values, enduring truth or the ultimate reality.

Q. What of philosophy?
A. Modern philosophy has lost cohesion and is now largely given over to introspection. Secular philosophy almost always reads the twilight as a preface to the dawn rather than as a prelude to deepening night, and so fails us when we most need help. It offers little guidance on priority issues, having fallen into massive confusion and contradiction. Much philosophy now debunks even reason itself, and that can only be self-destructive. The great systems of conjectural philosophy are spent and obsolete; the entire development of modern philosophy stands at a crossroads of uncertainty.

Q. How does your work square with the contemporary trend?
A. It is an argument for Christian beliefs in a time of spiritual shallowness and ethical confusion, a warning against what the current alternatives are doing to us and against the nihilism to which they lead, a presentation of the case for evangelical theism. It questions many of our generation's most cherished

assumptions and reaffirms the self-revealing God and the invincibility of his moral purposes.

Q. Why has theology been weak as an intellectual force during our century?

A. One can more readily forgive empirical science and conjectural philosophy for seeking to correlate reason only with changing phenomena and animalistic development than one can excuse recent Christian theology for dissociating reason from the Divine Logos, from the image of God in man, from rational divine revelation, from a scripturally-given truth of God. Neo-Protestant theologians needlessly impoverished reason and imperiled the case for Christian theism by stressing the volitions, emotions, existential decision, and other anti-intellectual alternatives. But religion raises no deeper question than whether we worship the true and living God or simply a deity of our own desiring. An intellectually persuasive case can be made for biblical theism, but neo-Protestant and neo-Catholic theology failed to make it.

Q. Do you then simply "write off" scientists and philosophers, even as many of them seem to have "turned off" theologians?

A. By no means. Every scientist and every philosopher sports a theology, although often a very shabby one, just as every last human being consciously or unconsciously lives by one. The first volume of my work devoted to "preliminary concerns" wrestles the interrelationships of theology, philosophy and science. My basic complaint is that recent big-name European theologians like Karl Barth and Rudolf Bultmann sealed off the discussion of God's self-revelation from the concerns of the scientist, the historian, and the philosopher—and thereby they impoverished all the disciplines of learning.

Q. Has theology a future?

A. Instead of being dismissed along with astrology and witchcraft (here we ought not to overlook the "Homeric gods" that scientists and philosophers frequently champion) theology will be recognized again before the end of this century as indispensably important. The day will soon come when even those clergy who thought it better to be social activists than theologians will concede that social change motivated by bromide-ideology leads to swift disenchantment; they will talk again about the kingdom of God, about God's revelation and righteousness and redemption, about the good news of the Gospel, as well as about justice and compassion. Laymen will again include serious theology in their reading. If our nation has a real future, political leaders too will have an eye on God in his revelation and declared purposes as much as on the pollsters and their prognostications.

Q. Do you see much to be thankful for this past year?

A. A great deal: That the Creator God lives and sustains the cosmos and man, and hence for life and food and shelter in a world insensitive to the fact that wickedness and injustice are doomed and that righteousness and love must ultimately prevail; for new life in Christ who died for our sins and is risen from the dead; for the Holy Spirit of God who renews broken and rebellious human beings and lifts us to personal fellowship and engages us for a world mission. I'm grateful that Christians can still make a difference in a world moving toward the End of All Ends and in a fast-declining nation not yet past redemption's point. The good news that God's grace can save us, can unleash a fresh tide of moral power and spiritual renewal, should be heralded from housetops, trumpeted on television, relayed on radio.

Q. Doesn't Christianity survive only underground in China and defensively in Eastern Europe and in Moslem lands? Isn't it virtually ignored as an intellectual option on most Western campuses? And even in the United States in this so-called "year of the evangelical" aren't evangelicals at odds?

A. You couldn't state this better. But things were worse when the Hebrews were slaves in Egypt, and when Christianity first came into the world, and Herod's political power-play aimed to massacre the Bethlehem infants and Pilate sent Jesus to the cross. But the God of the Bible is the God of the exodus and of the resurrection. He is the God who once lifted the pagan West to its nobler Christian heritage. He is the God of surprises. By the year 2000 the African continent may be half Christian. Asian Christians have commissioned a host of missionaries on that least Christian of the continents. Think of the many thousands of messianic Jews in America. And while Communist countries try unsuccessfully to eradicate Christianity the most powerful nation in the world has elected an evangelical Christian to the presidency. But one must speak with more qualification of the academic campuses and the mass media.

Q. Do you consider books as important as television in our media age?

A. The banality of television is driving more and more viewers to good reading. Books that confront the reigning ideas and ideals of an age are like earthquake tremors that signal impending disaster and prod people toward safer refuge. Neither television nor radio, governed by commercial instincts, "lends itself" to sustained reflection but is limited by sponsors' expectations of audience ratings and viewers' expectations of entertainment.

Q. Haven't the higher critics pretty well destroyed the Bible?

A. The Bible has destroyed more critical theories and humbled more critics than they would have you believe.

Q. But hasn't the modern world rather effectively neutralized God?

A. The Bible teaches the universal sinfulness of man, which means that every last one of us by moral revolt seeks to suppress God. But the Bible speaks of the self-revealing God, the living God who reveals himself in an amazing variety of ways: in the cosmos, in history, in the human mind and conscience, in the inspired Scriptures. In Jesus Christ he has come in person in an incarnate revelation. In every way except his final end-time revelation God has disclosed himself, and we may be grateful for the sake of those who still lack shelter from the coming storm that the final judgment of men and nations has not yet occurred. (*The Washington Star,* January 3, 1977.)

When he was a lad, Carl Henry stole a Bible while awaiting baptism in the Episcopal church in the U.S. Today he knows more about the Bible than almost anyone else alive. He got that way by reading his "hot" Bible, secretly at first, then compulsively. Reformed, he went on to become a newspaper editor, theology professor and prolific religion bookwriter. Today, Dr. Carl Henry, is known as "the most noted evangelical theologian in the U.S." He was given that title by Louis Cassels, late UPI religion editor and dean of U.S. religion writers.

Christian-Secular Battle Lines

Q. Dr. Henry, who and what is an evangelical, and how does he differ from a fundamentalist?
Dr. Henry. The term "evangelical" is preferable to the term fundamentalist for several reasons. If you ask me, do I believe in the great fundamentals of the Christian religion, the answer is, an unequivocal yes. But fundamentalism became a mood and a mentality as well. It arose as a reaction to Protestant modernism at the turn of the century. It had a one-sided interest in evangelism and got interested in social action only for the sake of evangelism and neglected the cultural and political arena. It also failed to address the mind of its generation. It dismissed all those in ecumenically related churches as apostate.

The term evangelical is superior because it has a biblical base. The apostle Paul tells us what the heart of the evangel is ... it is the Good News, that God forgives sinners, and gives new life based on Christ's substitutionary death and bodily resurrection in the context of a scripturally controlled message. Evangelicals are committed to what the Bible teaches. They are concerned for a vigorous defence of the faith and in sociocultural engagement.

Q. The relationship between culture and Christianity seems to be breaking down in North America. How do you view that?
A. There is a coalesence of two forces right now. On the one hand there is an accelerated decline of American culture morally and spiritually. On the other hand there is a dynamic upsurge of the evangelical movement with its demonstrated life transforming dynamic. These two trends happen just now to coincide and nobody can quite tell what the coalesence of those two trends will signify.

If the cultural decline continued and the acceleration of secularism persists, it could very well be that 'the ceiling is off,' of American greatness . . . the beginning of the end for America as a first-rate leading world power.

On the other hand we will not have an evangelical awakening in the U.S. simply by an increase of evangelistic activity that does not pose a challenge to the forces that are now shaping the public mentality and public life in America. Evangelicals are not shaping the public scene in America. The initiative belongs to the public campuses, public schools, colleges and universities.

Q. Where are the campuses intellectually today. The radical movements of the '60s seem dead.

A. The radically secular mood on campus becomes an occasion for these students to take a raincheck on their commitment to historic Christian beliefs. The predominant mood in the universities today, not that it's the majority view, is that everything is in change. All ideas, all religions, all philosophies, all moral imperatives are subject to the culture in which they arise.

For most, the idea of God, transcendent revelation and supernatural commandment is a pious fiction. Faith in a transcendent Savior has been jettisoned along with transcendent ethics and salvation.

Q. Where does the media fit into the secularizing process and where are its responsibilities?

A. The mass media are, along with the educational, the most potently powerful shapers of the ideals and attitudes of our generation. The media represent the rejection of Christian moral claims as evidence of progress and modernity. They do this, perhaps not intentionally, but because they don't preserve a challenge to the standpoint of modernity in the center of the mix, but on the margin of the mix. I view the mass media and God's revelation as being the two most powerful forces in history. The world, using communications as its medium, molds society by publicizing the "good life" with values which are generally contrary to God's principles. God, using Jesus Christ as his mediator, offers the best life.

Q. What do you see as the pressing issues between science and religion?

A. Man has lost faith in science or speculative reasoning as the source of a philosophy of life. Science may provide solutions for physical crises but the moral and spiritual decay of our generation will still exist. As the earth's existence is threatened, evangelical theology will regain popularity. Scientists foresee the world's doom from famine, over-population, pollution and nuclear war. The world is headed for disaster but these threats only skim the surface. The problem's root lies in the spiritual realm, not the physical.

Q. Where has religion, specifically Christianity and the churches, moved in the last decade?

A. There is a tremendous turn from the cover of *Time* magazine a few years ago with its front page: "Is God Dead?" to the *Newsweek* cover last year stating: "The Year of the Evangelical," which indicates something of what has happened.

The myth that supernatural religion has had its day, has itself passed, and we are seeing the outcropping of all forms of religion . . . from the evangelical Christian heritage to spiritism and a renewed interest in exorcism.

What troubles me about the enthusiasm that underlies the conviction that the day of the evangelical is here, is that it looks better because of the collapse of the alternatives. That could accommodate a misplaced confidence in the movement.

It looks better cosmetically because of the crisis of authority in Roman Catholicism which is in great disarray today. Large masses of Roman Catholics still attend their churches, nevertheless have broken in the realm of practical morality with the concept of the infallibility of the pope on the birth control issue. The crisis of authority has been further precipitated by an interest in sociology rather than in supernatural theology by some of its priests.

For the possibility of ordination of women priests, the idea of Mary as co-redemptrix, might in the near future be invoked. There are some intimations here and there that this might be on the margin of that move.

As the breakdown of authority in Roman Catholicism continues, we are, on the other hand seeing the breakdown of neo-Protestantism.

There is almost no enthusiasm going for ecumenism at the local level, and at the national level organized Christianity is in great confusion and retrenchment.

On the other side you place the evangelical movement with its publicly demonstrated evangelistic dynamic.

The fact that unlikely candidates for conversion like Charles Colson and Jeb Magruder and the "galloping gourmet" Graham Kerr belong to the media establishment, is significant. They stand in a line with a man like Saul of Tarsus, equally an unlikely candidate. And there's Eldridge Cleaver, who belongs to "the ugly Americans." These are people who have become bearers of the moral fortunes of our generation.

Q. The homosexual issue has been much in the news. What is the biblical position on this moral dilemma?

A. One has to say that Anita Bryant put her job on the line, but she has oversimplified the issues. The Christian churches are in turmoil on two issues. The evangelical wing sees more clearly than the non-evangelical wing, that homosexuality from the standpoint of the Bible is a sin, and ought not to be dismissed as a sickness. On the other hand they tend not to see the problem of civil rights, rights before the law. Non-evangelical churches see only the civil rights thing and lose the biblical judgment of wickedness and the possibility of redemption.

Q. There is increased skepticism about the reliability of the Bible as God's Word. Can we take the Bible seriously?

A. Only if we take it for what it really is—revelational truth.

Q. Can we take the Bible as literal truth?

A. The Bible is literally true in what it teaches about God and his relationship to man. There are anthropomorphisms, literary figures and much of the Bible is couched in poetry. Even the poetry of the Bible intends to say something literally true about God. When the biblical writers say God is a rock and uses a figure there is a cognitive reason for choosing that figure. He doesn't say God is a pebble. He conveys by the figure something that is cognitively true about God. When the Scripture says Jesus of Nazareth was born of a virgin, that he died for the sins of men and rose again, it presumes to tell us what is actually the case historically. (*The Vancouver Province*, July 9, 1977.)

Ever since he contributed the essay on "Science and Religion" to the volume titled *Contemporary Evangelical Thought* (1957), Arlington theologian Dr. Carl F.H. Henry has had a strong interest in the question of God and the cosmos. His newest symposium, *Horizons of Science: Christian Scholars Speak Out*, has just been published. Henry, founding editor of *Christianity Today* magazine, was interviewed by *Washington Star* Staff Writer William F. Willoughby.

Faith, Science Can Co-Exist

Q. Why are discussions of science and religion again commanding special interest?
Dr. Henry. There are several reasons. The question of God's revelation and relation to the world thrusts itself upon every generation. The evangelical upsurge reiterates the Judeo-Christian affirmation that God created and preserves the universe. Modern science and philosophy can't adequately explain man and the world on naturalistic premises. And contemporary scientists are baffled by the problem of origins.
Q. Then why did this fall into the background in the recent past?
A. Existential philosophy had much to do with this. Existentialism relates God, if at all, only to man's inner self, and allows naturalistic scientism undisputed rights to define the external world. The radically secular reduction of external reality to impersonal processes and events exiled God to the inner ghettos of personal faith. But philosophical existentialism is channeling into nihilism, and scientists themselves are discussing anew such topics as creation.
Q. But are their theories compatible with those of the religious?
A. Scientific observation and historical research are not competent to give a verdict on supernatural or transcendent relationships. But the Bible begins with the self-revealed God and it derives the world and man from him, and persuasively presents God as the providential preserver of the universe and as the merciful conveyor of redemptive grace to penitent sinners.
Q. Is science now more open to faith than in earlier decades?
A. Faith is no less an integral factor in scientific thought than in religious thought; indeed, faith is an element in all human understanding. Faith supplies the canopy idea that identifies, explains and evaluates data in which scientists or historians or theologians are interested. What distinguishes blind faith from genuine faith is the presence of verificational supports—non-

empirical or empirical—and the logical power or consistency attending explanatory principles. Biblical faith founds its verificational supports in the revealed Word of God; it claims that God in His revelation more comprehensively and consistently explains the data of being and life than any other alternative. All the evidence for order in the universe reflects God's activity and attests the givenness of nature. Philosophers of science increasingly concede that scientific theories are not the result of inductive inference; rather they are creative hypotheses that are tested empirically.

Q. What do you make of the widening scientific interest in extraterrestrial life and the efforts to establish communication with otherworldly intelligences?

A. It secretly witnesses to the fact that man is made for larger spheres of conversation than our planet shelters. Biblical religion focuses on the living God who speaks, and who takes the initiative in addressing His revelation to us. The Bible emphasizes that there are intelligible otherworldly creatures which exist that may be wiser than we are, angelic beings that love and serve God. The fact that modern man wants to initiate cosmic conversation on his own terms, and considers scientific formulas the nearest thing to wisdom and certainty, tells more about our generation than it does about the nature of reality.

Q. How do philosophers tend to view religion-and-science concerns?

A. There is little doubt that secular naturalism influentially prevails in the schools. Many think that God-talk is nonsense and they consider theology suspect. The radical secularists dismiss fixed truth and unchanging values; they consider truth and morality culture-relative and man an autonomous animal. Yet they curiously champion social justice, and the universal and permanent dignity of man and his individual worth, ecological responsibility, and much else. Such moral mandates cannot be consistently derived from the naturalistic creed. These ethical imperatives reflect the fact that, for all his naturalistic stance intellectually, modern man is linked still, even if in a broken way, to the divine image in man and to God in His revelation. He adjusts his day-to-day life to a higher sphere than statistical averages superimposed on a planet supposedly born of an explosion.

Q. Why haven't the churches mounted a more virile contribution to religion-and-science concerns?
A. Many public schools avoid the teaching of biblical theism as a sectarian prejudice while they accommodate the teaching of evolutionary humanism. Much of the organized church, which accommodated the "modern" scientific world view, tapered the Genesis account to moral generalizations; some exorcized the supernatural even from the gospels. Released-time religious education accommodated scientific humanism as the core of public school instruction, while it deployed to an optional leisure-time activity the probing of supernatural theism.
Q. What impact has education had on the younger generation?
A. The universities have given them a staggering amount of information about empirically observed phenomena. But they have failed the younger generation intellectually in respect to spiritual reality and proffer no agreed moral values. They have on the whole provided no firm alternative to the moral relativism of our age; while they nourish concern for social justice and especially for racial equality, they do so in the absence of a world life view that effectively anchors these or any other human values. The remarkable thing is that, for all the non-theistic orientation of most liberal learning, the most virile Christian witness has emerged from college and university youth who have found biblical vitalities outside their classroom studies and who now spiritually outpace many of their professors.
Q. Do you not then take a very skeptical view of science?
A. Not at all. It can be pursued to the glory of God or in the service of the demonic, as we well know. Scientific theory becomes the haven of many false gods, especially in an age that forsakes the living God. The fact of causality was long dogmatically affirmed by physicists, and with much less justification, than the affirmation of God by the theologians. The scientist has on the basis of empirical method no legitimate metaphysics at all. I take a dim view of anything—science, philosophy, theology, the nation, mankind and myself—if it's in the service of false gods. (*The Washington Star*, February 23, 1978.)

Dr. Henry, a noted theologian, author and lecturer, was the founding editor of *Christianity Today*, and now is lecturer-at-large for World Vision International. He was interviewed for the *Presbyterian Journal* while presenting a series of lectures on the authority of Scripture last spring at Covenant College.

Why Christians Differ Politically

Q. Dr. Henry, you are a man with a feel for the pulse of the evangelical world. In this political year, we seem to have polarized around groups like Moral Majority on the right and Evangelicals for Social Action on the left. Can a Jerry Falwell and a John Anderson ever hope to stand together before the American public and say convincingly that what they hold in common as Christians—even what they hold politically as Christians—transcends their differences? In other words, is there any possibility of pulling together the two extremes which we see among evangelicals?

Dr. Henry. I don't know. I think there was a time when the magazine *Christianity Today* might have served as a catalyst which would have so stimulated evangelical interest in sociopolitical and cultural impact that it might have led the way toward constructive conversations about evangelical objectives in public life. We needed to discuss goals, principles, platforms, priorities, particular candidates and specific legislation.

But evangelicals by and large have neglected a comprehensive policy of socio-political and cultural involvement and have tended instead to get in only on specifics. It is too easy, for example, to put John Anderson and Mark Hatfield into the same "liberal" basket just because they happen to agree on a few specifics to which conservatives object. In fact, there are vast differences between them on the issue of the role of the military and with regard to the essential integrity of the political process.

But yes—we do seem to have fragmented, and there is not one Christian voice. We lack any platform for bringing evangelicals together for a look at themselves. We also lack a basis for asking the important questions in a comprehensive and orderly way.

In a way, this is parallel to the predicament evangelicals face on the issues of inerrancy, inspiration and authority. I think there *could* have been cooperation among evangelicals on these matters at one time if each evangelical had been asked to spell out what, within his area of commitment, would advance the claims of the Bible as over against the secular world.

Now I don't mean that such minimal viewpoints are solid enough, for example, that our Christian colleges and seminaries can be effectively built on them. But I do mean that it is inexcusable to drive out of the evangelical community good scholars (like F.F. Bruce on the matter of inerrancy, for example) simply because they don't identify themselves wholly with what most evangelicals might consider normative.

All this has happened on the issue of inerrancy. The same thing is happening on the political front. That deeply troubles me.

Q. But is there any possibility of going back far enough so that we can start over and then begin speaking—or perhaps even *more* important, start thinking—together as evangelical Christians in the area of politics?

A. Once more, there seems to be an overwhelming tendency to get involved first in the specifics.

There seems, for example, to be an increasing feeling that we ought to have something like a Christian political party, even if it doesn't carry that specific name or label. But Christians need to realize the implications of exercising that kind of political clout (whether through a formal party or through the political action groups which have recently been formed by evangelicals) both in terms of principle and in terms of strategy.

In terms of principle, it would invite blaming evangelical Christianity for all kinds of mistakes. It would also raise the basic question of how religious beliefs ought to be translated into specific political programs, rather than maintained as mere principles or policies.

Q. In a year when many evangelicals will look at a candidate and ask how he stands on abortion, how he voted on SALT II, what position he took on the Panama Canal—how do you advise a Christian to size up a candidate?

A. Well, I would certainly go beyond those issues.

I would advise evangelicals, for example, to invite someone involved in the SALT II negotiations to sit down and

Why Christians Differ Politically 55

discuss with them what the limited objectives of the treaty are and how they fit into the more comprehensive program of American international strategy.

Likewise, someone who has supported the Panama Canal treaty. Whether one agrees with him or not, it is important to ask him within what framework he may have supported the treaty. For example, what if a particular senator supported it because he also believed he recognized some longstanding commitment to the construction of another, far more modern, canal in some other Central American country—but for various reasons was unable to speak publicly about that long term commitment? Now you still might not agree with him, but at least you would begin to realize he has a reason for voting for the treaty which you might not have thought of before.

Q. What positively should you look for in a candidate?
A. First of all, personal integrity. Irrespective of a person's convictions, his performance is unpredictable without personal integrity. Now while a Christian is not, just because of that fact, necessarily preferable as a candidate, at least the fact that he is a Christian—and acts by his convictions—should make his behavior generally predictable.

I think, incidentally, that the distinction between a person's private morality and his public morality is an illicit one. It is impossible to draw a rigid line between the two.

Second, and no less important than moral integrity, is the matter of political competence. When we go to a doctor, and are in need of emergency treatment, we do not go to someone who is inexperienced in the realm of those particular maladies, but to a specialist. We need to look for political competence and experience, and this is what greatly troubles me about those who think we should send only Christians to Congress. I can certainly think of instances in which it would be possible for a nonevangelical to be far more qualified politically to perform a particular task.

Back when I was editor of *Christianity Today*, someone asked me if I would support the Prohibition Party candidate for President. I asked whom the candidate would name as secretary of state—and he looked at me as if I were a heel, for he didn't have any idea. You just can't separate the Presidency from its international and domestic obligations and focus on just one issue.

A third criterion to use in measuring a candidate is the whole range of principles and national policies that he is identified with, and the priorities by which he organizes those policies and principles. Here I think evangelicals have done the least spadework. Let me say once more: They leap over principles, policy, platform and go immediately to specifics—either to specific candidates or to specific issues like bussing, abortion or something else.

Now I need to say that specific issues are not unimportant. They can be terribly important. For instance, the American conscience needs to be aroused over the inhumane slaughter of millions of unborn fetuses.

Q. Can you give a couple of examples of those root principles which ought to serve as guidelines for evangelicals as they think about specific candidates and issues?

A. I think human rights is a fundamental issue. Certainly those who stand in a democracy—most of all Christians—ought not to neglect the imperative of human rights before the world.

At the same time, there is the danger, which we have seen in President Carter's administration, of making human rights the only determining factor in international relations. In doing so we neglect what is also important—questions of security and economic survival. There is a delicate balance. President Carter now has had to pull back from a rather uncritical view of human rights which was quite moralistic rather than politically sanguine. He now has virtually sacrificed his earlier priorities on the human rights emphasis and diluted them to lesser concerns.

Q. Which he might not have had to do had he been more balanced in the first place?

A. Exactly.

Q. So you would list security and economic survival as worthy goals for a Christian seeking criteria by which to judge a candidate?

A. Yes, exactly. Think about inflation. I think *Christianity Today* was probably the only religious journal, and the first religious journal, to come out with an editorial to the effect that inflation is a moral evil. It's going to carry us down. I remember J. Howard Pew saying to me once, "Young man, not before I die, but before you die, you will be paying $100 for what is now available for $1."

If you want a further question about political integrity, watch the extent to which a candidate or an officeholder is more concerned with image than with realities. That is one of the pernicious aspects of contemporary life that is accelerated by the mass media.

Q. Are you basically an optimist or a pessimist?

A. I'm very optimistic about the Gospel and about Christianity, especially in terms of its missionary and evangelistic thrusts. I think the third great era of world missions may be in the making. In contrast with the first era, when pioneer missionaries went to target countries, and in contrast with the second era when the missionary cause was closely associated with colonial expansion, today we have task forces ready to go to every single part of the world. Even the non-Western churches are becoming missionary-sending churches.

There are doors opening in China. Even if they are opening only because of the pragmatic tactical commitments of Marxism, that is not really the point, because for now the doors do seem to be opening. There's hope in that area.

What troubles me is that the evangelical community seems pretty much reconciled to the collapse of Western culture. I don't see any reason for reconciling ourselves to the early extinction of Western culture as we have known it due mainly to the threat posed by the predator Communist nations.

We have a lot to learn from Solzhenitsyn, even if he does understate the values which have survived in the West somewhat. He is at least more discerning of our vulnerabilities than many Westerners are.

Q. You have a broader perspective than some of us do, due to the length of your service in God's kingdom. What do you see as the high points of the evangelical contribution during your lifetime?

A. The impact of Billy Graham in evangelism, penetrating across denominational lines and into the ecumenical arena, has set up a process of reverse challenge and momentum which had been lost through the earlier emergence of the powerful ecumenical bloc in western Christianity.

Second, I would point to the formation of *Christianity Today*, which provided an intellectual and cohesive framework under which evangelicals could unite and through which they could reach with increasing confidence into some areas of public involvement as well as theological.

Third, the world congresses on evangelism—especially the first one in Berlin. There was a coming together of theological and evangelistic concerns in a larger sense than had happened before. By the time of the second congress in Lausanne, the concern had shifted to Christianity's social impact—something to which *Christianity Today* itself contributed. Unfortunately, the door was left quite wide open to the ambiguity of the rival views which were presented. But there was also greater lay involvement at Lausanne, and the power of the lay movement is being reflected in many parts of Christianity now.

On the constructive side, there is the fact that the whole evangelical movement has passed beyond the stance of the uneasy conscience of modern fundamentalism with its fear of compromise which was so prevalent at mid-century. There was the feeling that to get publicly involved might be to destroy ourselves.

Q. And what have been evangelicalism's failings?

A. We're terribly confused—and that's a great tragedy. Various wings keep trying to define this or to define that, but no one really has a platform for doing so. One group tries it, and then another group tries it, and whatever wing tries it first is then maligned by some other wing. Nobody transcends the whole situation.

The other great disappointment to me is the failure of evangelicals to establish a Christian university. I think we will look back on this and see that this deprived the nation of a great intellectual platform for the critical assessment of modern evangelical views and the elaboration of evangelical Christianity in all the dimensions of modern thought.

Q. You state that as if it is no longer possible.

A. I think economically it is no longer feasible. As a matter of fact, the established evangelical colleges that once spoke secretly of becoming Christian universities increasingly have difficulties meeting their existing budgets. (*The Presbyterian Journal*, September 24, 1980.)

One of Carl F.H. Henry's many books, *The Uneasy Conscience of Modern Fundamentalism*, **prods Bible-believing Christians to take social responsibilities more seriously. The book is regarded by many Christian leaders as having been used by God to motivate evangelicals toward greater involvement in the world around them. Dr. Henry, president of the American Theological Society, lives in the Washington, D.C. area. He is highly respected for his spiritual insights on the American scene. This interview with him focuses upon concerns with election-year significance.**

Morals and Politics

Our heritage of values and the interface of the church with our world.

Q. Our country has on the one hand a Judeo-Christian heritage and on the other hand a commitment to church-state separation. To what extent are we justified in seeking to impose our views as Christians upon others—even such broad concepts as justice?

Dr. Henry. The Constitution forbids the making of any law "respecting an establishment of religion, or prohibiting the free exercise thereof." Many have misused these words to eclipse our Judeo-Christian heritage. Some would even twist them to promote secular humanism as an almost official religion. Even American politics is badly infected by pragmatism and relativism. What is right and good and true one day may be thrown out the next.

Judeo-Christian convictions are based on eternal principles, and those who hold them have as much right as others to promote their views in a pluralistic society like ours. Justice, moreover, is not self-defining. Communists define it one way (what the rulers wish), Khomeini another, some other Muslim leaders still another, Hindus who consider the fate of the poor an unalterable divine given another, while the Bible defines it as the self-revealing God proclaims it to be.

The living God has *established* civil government to preserve and apply justice (not to define or redefine it), and to promote peace. The task of Christians is to proclaim and exemplify God's righteousness, not to impose it by arbitrary political power upon others (who often do not hesitate to impose their unacceptable views on Christians). We are to address the conscience of the community by precept, practice and proclamation, until the citizenry voluntarily judges itself by, and acknowledges the rightness of laws that conform to the principles by which Christ will ultimately judge all men and nations.

Q. Even foes of the prayer amendment concede that the Supreme Court has not banned prayer and Bible reading in public schools but only forbids government-mandated devotional exercises. Yet because some educators are using the decision not only to prohibit prayer and Bible reading but in some places to outlaw Christmas carols and baccalaureates, what would be the problem of a constitutional amendment affirming the right to pray?

A. My view is that the center of the storm is the content of classroom teaching, not devotions on the margin. Evangelicals would quickly disown a college that opened classes with prayers to God and then proceeded to teach humanism to students. Regrettably, evangelicals have not pressed through the breach which was left deliberately by the Schempp decision that permits teaching the Bible as history and literature. It's easier to organize a postcard protest against banning prayer; even some folk who don't attend church prayer meetings will join the cause. Keep prayer in the schools even if it dwindles in the churches! To be sure, the Supreme Court has unjustifiably paid less attention to encroachments on personal freedom than to reinforcing the "nonestablishment" clause. Voluntary prayer should not be discouraged, while the issue of Christmas carols may best be resolved by parents at each local level. Bible reading in public schools is another matter. Even better would be to teach the Bible as literature and history with fair recognition of its own claims. Secular teachers have no license to superimpose a nontheistic philosophy, and evangelical colleges that cannot equip student teachers to teach the Bible competently and acceptably should ask why not. Students brought up in orthodox homes (Jewish, Catholic or Protestant) are improperly taught at home if they cannot raise the right questions in the public classroom.

Q. Is a humanistic or naturalistic orientation necessarily bad?

A. Humanism can provide no objective basis for what it considers good or bad; such conceptions are open to constant revision. Christians can, however, cooperate with humanists when humanists happen to espouse proper concerns (neighbor love, conservation of energy), yet we should not commend their tenuous humanist supports. I might add that the humanist's ethical commitments have no logical basis apart from Scriptural teaching. They borrow biblical principles without crediting their source. The Bible teaches that the humanist knows more than he admits: the living God is revealed to all mankind. Humanist rejection of the supernatural, in short, is due not to a lack of evidence but basically to a rebellion of the will.

Q. Who are the real heroes of our time?
A. The real heroes of our time are those who in a faithless age hold, live and share their faith in God. Genuine revolutionary courage belongs to those who remain true to God even if atheistic rulers force them underground or punish citizens simply for being Christians. The true immortals will be those who seek to apply the principles of the Bible concretely to the complicated realities of modern life, who preserve a devout and virtuous family life, who are faithful to the abiding values of yesterday, today and tomorrow. If our lives are undisciplined by God's truth and our hearts untuned to God's premises, we shall be beset by hopeless illusions.

Q. How does the world most notably affect the life of the church today?
A. A race that is radically corrupt, to which we too are linked even if we now belong to Christ, threatens to ensnare us by its constant misperceptions of life, freedom, power, love, hope and much else. We live in a disoriented society. Vast multitudes think they escape measurement by an absolute simply because they affirm that no absolute exists and follow their gut-instincts. Many influential educators, under whom the young study, have no serious interest in revealed religion and lack effective sanctions to curtail the seething corruption of our age. Even well-intentioned politicians make a slogan of self-determination; they rightly challenge predatory nations but obscure God's moral sovereignty in history. Love of self then readily replaces love of God and neighbor. In such a generation all the explorations of science can be deployed by pagan profligates in the service of evil. Our society's main source of high culture is television, which replaces the cruelties

of the Roman amphitheater by programmed violence and dignifies immorality with theatrical subtlety. The titillated masses eagerly scramble aboard this pre-routed cattle car that transports them free of charge to an intellectual Auschwitz. For a half-hour prime-time soap opera they exchange the hard-won moral heritage of the ages. So, a fantastically powerful medium conditions "mature" audiences to ethical permissiveness, while humanists insist in the schools that coming of age requires the rejection of the God of the Bible, revealed truth, and the inherited virtues as primitive taboos.

Q. Then what hope is there for the younger generation?

A. A great deal, if they avoid the fallacies of their elders and learn from the wisdom of the ages, most of all the Scriptures. The young—more quickly than they suspect—are candidates for middle age and old age, and the precious twenties are gone like a summer night. Think of Jesus beginning his own public ministry just before he turned 30, choosing disciples from those in that age bracket, and enlisting them for an awesome world mission. What would he say today to those for whose approbation politicians and professors aspire, flattering them by declarations of their incomparable importance to the modern world: "Don't deprive civilization of your potential!"

Would Jesus not warn them of the house built on sand—and that their fondest dreams may well turn into a bag of wind? Would he not call them to refine their ideals and values—love, freedom, hope, happiness—lest they fall into the trap of irrational counterfeits? Would he not warn them against tradition—against the legacy that even many of their elders have left them? Would he not speak plainly of sin and shame and repentence and real life and freedom? Would he not warn them of the evils and temptations of society that have beguiled a parent generation, and that carry the youth generation in turn perilously near the gates of hell? Would he not say they are right in much of their protest, yet condemned by their own failure to find the better way, the narrow way, that leads to the Cross where Jesus manifested love even in his death, and where the penitent can find the glorious liberty of the children of God? Would he not speak to them of liberating truth, power, love and joy, and enlist them, as he did Peter, John and James, in a world-wide mission that involves the destiny of all humans?

Q. What is the spiritual temper of the campuses?
A. No two are alike. But very much an exception are those where spiritual and moral vitalities permeate the academic curriculum. For its disinterest in the Judeo-Christian revelation modern learning pays an exhorbitant price, the loss of fixed truths and transcendent values, and of cohesive, integrated education. No consensus exists on who or what or if God is, no spectrum of widely shared values survives, no agreed basis of objective authority is adduced. The collapsing conscience of Western youth consequently becomes a shambles. But on the edge of the classrooms there appear many evangelical influences and movements; in these one finds most of what spiritual vigor there is. However, among evangelicals intellectual interests, in contrast with devotional priorities, are often disappointingly weak. Yet one must mention the emergence in the secular academic milieu of a competent vanguard of Christian philosophers, and this cadre of theistic academics is making its presence felt even on some of the nation's major campuses and is challenging the existential mood.

Another encouraging sign is the refusal of a large multitude of students to accept the premises of secular humanism as decisive for their own commitments. A gratifying number of students have turned to Christ, received the forgiveness of sins and new spiritual life, not indeed as a result of classroom content but rather often despite it. This evangelical student movement has become the most dynamic evangelistic force in many church congregations.

Q. In what ways are college students changing?
A. Many are now asking what values their professors affirm, and why. More and more consider college education not as a gateway to intellectual finalities but rather as a gateway to a more lucrative job, a prospect that now often goes unfulfilled. Those who have been exposed to the biblical heritage at home recognize that the West no longer gives its children a Christian education; inside or outside the communist orbit, public learning seems intellectually antichrist. Most academics studiously avoid classroom reference to Jesus Christ—understandably so: for to mention Christ in a formative way would only put intellectual and moral world-wisdom on the defensive. Academe tends therefore un-

protestingly to allow the rabble and the radicals to recrucify him. More and more students see no convincing basis for humanistic ethical commitments in a naturalistic view of the cosmos and man and, except as some probe anew the reality of God, they make materialistic priorities the chief end of life. Some traditionally religious colleges have swallowed humanist philosophy to the point of gastritis; mention significant works on theology and their students are tempted to reach for a sleeping pill. Students with clearly defined spiritual and moral concerns tend to be either orthodox Jews, Roman Catholics, or evangelicals.

Q. What are some of the unquestioned prejudices of our time?

A. The intellectual idolatries are many, all the more ironically because they are cherished by those who have no patience with revealed religion, fixed truths, eternal commandments. The one "unthinkable" prospect of our technological society is (not the possibility of scientific destruction of modern civilization, for that prospect would congratulate the power potential of the scientific community, but rather) *divine doom!* The Second Coming of Christ, the End of all ends, the gates of hell, the resurrection of the dead, the final judgment of mankind—these are ruled out by the wisdom of the world. Once one subconsciously subscribes to this agenda of intellectual "no no's" the good, the right, the ideal, the true, the just, the fine, the noble become less significant than the new, the spectacular, the quantitatively grandiose. So there arises a herd of humanity that anesthetizes the possibilities of spiritual life and knifes itself to spiritual death, a generation with mustard-seed consciences, a society that believes in pseudovalues and pseudotruths. What our society needs, it implies, is not more churches but more television sets. The promise of a creative new American culture looms with the "wedding game" on prime time TV, the pornographic seduction of art so we can draw from *Playboy* and from X-rated films the inspiration for a society that makes less use of its mental organs than of its sexual organs, until sex is the atomic mushroom that reduces Western man to an exhausted monster. Sexual deviations that two generations ago only psychotics disclosed privately to psychologists have now become consciously espoused lifestyles. We have science to dispel our fears of pregnancy, or to abort an unintended launching of life; what need of Christ to dispel the darkness? But a terrible future judgment awaits our scientific culture that eagerly purges itself of belief in God.

Q. What current affirmations do you question?

A. We constantly hear—from politicians who themselves want to be perceived as good—that human beings, especially Americans, are intrinsically good. Another is that democratic government is benevolent, when it is really becoming a bureaucratic monster that we seem unable to cage. Third-World nations are misled into believing that politicians can miraculously turn their famine into bread and their drought into wine. Another cliché is that God is never critical of the poor, or that the West—and not the finitude of earthly resources—is mainly to blame for world poverty. Still another adage is that capitalism is degrading while socialism is ennobling. Another is that military muscle is the main key to world influence.

The dilemmas that confound our leaders actually tell us much about the stupidities of our civilization with its moral facades and spiritual evasions. Military preparedness may indeed be a necessary deterrent in an age of predator powers. But any nation that thinks God may be tempted to evaporate because of this vast armory of destructive might has in store a might surprise when resurrection morning unveils that omnipotent judge of the nations. The masses too are prone to think that a cosmetician can best enhance individual personality, that life's prime asset is sexual allure. Alongside this, they rank material affluence as the god worthy of all energies. Our adults bequeath these unquestionable profundities to their children in what is really a betrayal of the younger generation.

Q. Some say that our current drift toward socialism has been encouraged by Christian indifference, the decline of voluntarism, and a general lack of responsible teaching by churches and Christian schools. Would you agree?

A. Instead of being indifferent to socialism, some Christian churchmen early in this century fell over each other in their rush to declare Jesus a socialist; some naively repeat the error today. If, however, you mean indifference to capitalist injustices, inadequate teaching here too is a factor. Many evangelical schools failed to vindicate the values of capitalism and also failed to criticize its sins; thus they created an undeserved sympathy for socialism which consequently appeared benevolent. Many victims of socialism today would like to escape to capitalist countries. The real welcome for socialism lay in a tendency to discount what the Bible actually teaches. The decline of voluntarism, the selfish desire to claim what others have without working for it and without in turn sharing it with others who have less, is a contributory factor.

Q. What's your answer to the problems of poverty and hunger around the world? Do you feel that any substantial progress is possible in the next few years? If so, will it be at the expense of environmental concerns?

A. There's something of a cruel hoax in the suggestions now often heard that a simplified life style by Western Christians could end world poverty and hunger. Third World countries do not wish to hear the hard news that the finiteness of earthly resources limits human possibilities of universal affluence, although petrol problems have begun to carry a message. The rise of the Euroamerican middle class is a remarkable exception in history, not a norm, and it imposed special stewardship opportunities and responsibilities upon Western Christians, especially in respect to the world missionary enterprise and humanitarian needs. Doubtless all humans will soon be forced, by inflation and other problems, to a simpler life style, and Christians have spiritual incentives beyond the economic necessities for an avoidance of elaborate living. Everyone must feel an obligation to the needy neighbor at his side. But Christians have a powerful motivation for doing so in their awareness that all mankind bears God's creation-image, and that Christ died for all. American Christians have been singularly benevolent, although we still have much to learn about sacrifice. Yet many are responding to global world needs through voluntary agencies like World Vision that emphasize not only emergency relief but the development of voluntary programs abroad that cope long-range with local problems. The wealthier nations, at least in the Free World, have also felt an economic responsibility for helping impoverished nations. Helping the destitute is a duty of every human everywhere who has more than his neighbor has.

Q. Inasmuch as the New Testament gives no indication that Jesus or Paul ever engaged in what we would call social action, what rationale is there for the Christian today to get involved?
A. The New Testament, properly interpreted. Jesus lived out Isaiah 61, inscribing that passage on messianic liberation over his public ministry (Luke 4:17ff), although he postponed beyond the present church age "the day of vengeance" when the Lord will implement universal justice by transcendent force. By his sinless life Jesus triumphed over all the powers of evil, and by his bodily resurrection he vanquished all the oppressive and exploitative powers that would have destroyed him. Since his crucifixion and resurrection all the powers of injustice are dated and doomed. We are to proclaim *all* that Jesus taught, including the requirements of justice by which at his coming Christ will judge the nations, and bannering the Gospel of forgiveness and new life to all who believe.

The Risen Lord declared that "all authority" had been given to him; nobody therefore has license to exercise authority as an independent prerogative unanswerable to him. The Gospel pledges man's deliverance from his total need and comprehends a new society of the twice-born over whom Christ rules. As to the apostle Paul, what could be more dramatic as a matter of social involvement than his insistence that not Caesar whom the Romans worshiped but Christ is Lord: "one Lord" (Eph. 4:5)? Yet Paul appealed to Caesar for justice (Acts 25:11). His classic chapter (Rom. 13) stresses God's ordination of civil government for justice and order, and that Christians are to support the ends God wills in and through it. Paul's letter to Philemon about Onesimus "a brother beloved" (v. 16), moreover, sounds the death-knell of slavery.

Q. Do you see the Bible as predicting a continuation of wars? If so, what motivation is there to work for peace?
A. The Bible indicates that sin will continue until the final end of human history, and apostasy grow worse and worse, yet that is no reason for acquiescing in it and abandoning ourselves to it. The motivation to strive for peace lies in the fact that Christ is the Prince of Peace, of a comprehensive peace that deals with the grim realities of sin and death, with reconciliation among men and reconciliation to God. Short-sighted humans, unwilling to pay the spiritual cost of such

peace, instead spend themselves bankrupt for military hardware on the assumption that cold war is the best that mankind can hope for. War is not the best we can hope for but, as Jesus indicated, it is the sad actuality that an unregenerate race is likely to inherit and invite. For all that, war is not inevitable in the sense that the final judgement of an arbitrary nation is divine given; it is suspended upon human decision. In a day of dread nuclear power Christians should eagerly pursue a delay of hostilities as a welcome context for promoting Christ's claims. Yet war is not the worst of all evils; an unwillingness to live and die for truth and right is, since this is individually self-destructive and a betrayal of human dignity.

Q. How do you see 2 Chronicles 7:14 applying to Americans in the 1980's? How can I as an individual be expected to repent for social wrongs over which I have had little or no control?

A. Promises to the Hebrew theocracy are not automatically transferable to the nations at large. We Americans are not God's covenant people. America has, in any event, no biblical guarantee of perpetuity. Even God's grace universally respects the foundations of his moral order; Jerusalem was eventually sacked by the Babylonians as a punishment for the sins of the people. Yet it is true also that God in sovereign mercy often spares a nation for the sake of a righteous remnant, to provide another season for repentance and spiritual renewal. But does a Christian remnant really stand in the gap today, agonizing over the nation's sins, pleading with God to delay punishment for one more possible turning-time in the life of the people? As to personal involvement in the deeds of another, the whole principle of racial guilt in Adam our representative is predicated upon it, and likewise it is presupposed in the possibility of our personal justification on the ground of Christ's representational life and death in the sinner's stead. God deals with human beings not only individually but corporately, and our involvement in collective and national guilt is one of the aspects of this. (*Christian Herald*, October 1980.)

To pursue the influence of the intellectuals among evangelicals, *Eternity* interviewed Carl F.H. Henry at his Arlington, Virginia, home. Henry qualifies as the dean of evangelical scholars. Holding twin doctorates (Th.D., Northern Baptist and Ph.D. in philosophy, Boston University), he is currently the president of the American Theological Society and a member of Cosmos Club, a nonreligious intellectual fellowship. As the founding editor of *Christianity Today*, Henry set the standard for attention to academic credentials, broad evangelical strategy, downplay of petty differences, and concern for the larger American culture.

Making of a Christian Mind

Q. Why is there a relative lack of intellectuals among evangelicals, as compared to, say, Jewish, Roman Catholic, or liberal-Protestant groups?

Dr. Henry. The evangelicals have never achieved a great national evangelical university. Instead, they have emphasized evangelism and missions as the ideal Christian career. These factors, I think, have made a situation in which evangelical achievement in the broad world of learning and of human service is more the exception than the rule.

Q. You have long pushed for a Christian university. What was it that you felt limited Christian colleges so that you wanted to start yet another one?

A. None of the existing colleges was truly a university. A university is composed of a plurality of colleges, each offering specialized studies in a particular area, so that under the orbit of the one university there would be a college of law and science and philosophy and communications—the whole spectrum. The tremendous cost of scientific equipment would probably limit the ability of a Christian university to do much in the physical sciences without huge government grants. But we thought a great deal could be done with philosophy of science in a Christian university.

Q. Do you feel that a school like Oral Roberts has a crack at what you have envisioned? They do have a law school, a medical school, and so on.

A. Yes, I think in a smaller way. It is not a national university, and it does not draw into its orbit all the streams of evangelical intellectual power. Actually it's become more noteworthy for its basketball team than for its other features. But Roberts did singlehandedly what the evangelical community did not do: he planted a university of a certain dimension and showed that it could be done.

The great asset of Christian learning can be that it expounds fixed truths and a life-changing dynamic in a day when secular learning seems unable to cope with moral relativity and social revolution and violence. Sound Christian learning will make a solid case for the God of creation and redemption and judgment, and for objective truth and moral finalities. For all that, many evangelical centers too much neglect the Christian mind. The Bible is a brilliant, relevant light, but it can be focused to discourage hard investigation in areas where Scripture conveys no information—the complex structure of the universe, for example. The Christian mind should seek analytical skill and comprehensive illumination on the critical issues of our time.

Q. Looking over the last 100 years of evangelical history you can see ebbs and flows, periods when the evangelical movement was stronger intellectually, or placed a higher priority on thinking, and periods when it was weaker. Where are we now?

A. The magnificent penetration that Billy Graham got at midcentury into the mainline denominations helped rescue evangelicals from their "fundamentalist ghetto" image. Yet the surge of enthusiasm for evangelism on many evangelical campuses and the existential mood of American life worked against a deep, stable, intellectual interest on the campuses. We are only beginning to see some of the consequences. The careful distinctions that were so important in the thirties in the world of evangelical thought are now blurred and critical theological analysis is hard to come by.

Q. You feel then we are in a "down time"?

A. Yes. I had hoped that there would come out of the seventies a real theological awakening among evangelicals. Francis Schaeffer has done some intermediary spade work in enlisting intellectual interest, but the movement has really not deepened its ideas or seriously engaged with the academic crossfire.

Q. What is involved in that crossfire?

A. I think humanism, the awakening Jewish community with counter-Christian claims, the Moslem community in its growing political and intellectual significance—in all of these I have a feeling the evangelicals are far less ready than they ought to be.

Q. There is more activity and aggressiveness, however.

A. Yes, but we risk approaching politics, or the mass media, or the intellectual dilemma on a "quick fix" basis.

Q. Give us an example of something you consider a "quick fix."

A. Well, the whole matter of the world of learning, the world of ideas. We aren't going to change the humanistic orientation of the American school system by preserving private prayer in the public schools.

Q. What about the influence of Christian television, especially the political impact?

A. Evangelicals have been looking for leadership, and they've been woefully deprived of it. This makes it possible for a charismatic personality with access to the media to serve as a rallying point for the discontent of many people.

Q. How do you respond to the statement, "Christ is the answer for our society"?

A. That is overly simplistic. It is in principle right, but it is overly simplistic when applied to specifics, because there are many specific, critical issues of contemporary culture to which the Bible gives no specific answer. It doesn't tell you whether to go ahead with nuclear energy or not, or to build a certain bomb or not. But it gives you principles. And in the light of those principles, we seek the preferable alternative among the various live options available. Now that may seem very distressing to the person who wants only absolutes and thinks it's a waste of time to deal with probability. But life in the political order is like that, and in the political order we are not bringing in the kingdom of God.

Q. What were some of the influences in your own intellectual development?

A. I think the fact that I took a course in the history of philosophy and I majored in philosophy in college; and the fact that I got under a good philosophy teacher, Gordon Clark, who refused to give us answers until we literally hurt with the questions. He made us see how one view arose in order to respond to another's intellectual weaknesses, and he did not quickly include Christian ideas. That makes for good internal analysis. Evangelicals are woefully weak at internal analysis. They tend to leap quickly to "the Bible says."

Secondly, the fact that Wheaton in those days had a

course in theism and ethics required of all seniors. The textbook was James Orr's *Christian View of God and the World* and that was a mind-stretching experience.

Then, too, I went to college primarily to get an education. I became interested in books, an expensive investment, but I have learned they are good friends. Another thing is that I have consciously sought out good scholars across lines, and frontier scholars within the evangelical community as well, for dialogue and exchange.

Q. What counsel did you give your children about their schooling?

A. I did not thrust an evangelical college upon them. If they would learn God's will about their life vocations, I said, we would help them meet the cost of college or university studies, with these agreements: First, they should feel free to study anywhere in the world, preferably under the best teachers in their field, with the single provision that they identify themselves with Christian student work on campus. Then, if they were to marry during undergraduate studies, we would assume they could also carry their own tuition costs. The latter restriction was to encourage the easiest fulfillment of possible later postgraduate studies.

As it happened, both our children completed undergraduate studies at Wheaton. After a stint in the Peace Corps our son, Paul, finished doctoral studies in political science at Duke, and he currently is serving in the Michigan State Legislature. Our daughter, Carol, received her doctorate from Indiana University School of Music; she is now teaching in the music department at University of South Carolina.

Q. What can you tell us about the Institute for Advanced Christian Studies which you and other scholars began in the sixties?

A. It's a modest "triple fall-back" from the Christian university ideal, yet retains some real intermediary values. First we had hoped to sponsor a think-tank where a rotating core of mature evangelical scholars would work side by side to complete their major works. But we couldn't attract $350,000 to buy Haverford Hotel outside Philadelphia as a center. The higher the academic vision, the less evangelical monetary enthusiasm there is. But a matching gift from Lilly Endowment enabled us, as a further fall-back, to provide grants of $10,000 to $16,000 to evangelical scholars who proposed urgently needed volumes that they assured us they could complete in good time (not all have).

Q. What projects were completed?

A. Outstanding is a two-volume history of Asian Christianity that the distinguished American missionary to Korea, Samuel Hugh Moffett, is completing; the first volume is finished. Already in print are Stephen Monsma's *The Unraveling of America* (on politics), Gilbert Bilezikian's *The Gospel of Mark and Greek Tragedy*, and numerous other volumes, and a considerable number of monographs or articles in technical journals. An important work on the problem of evil is in process. But we enlisted too few of the best scholars, and on rather uncoordinated topics at that. For that reason IFACS shifted to a third strategy.

We have charted major clashpoints between Christianity and the modern secular outlook and have proceeded with consultants to invite scholars most competent to formulate the Christian view in a series of college paperback texts. These scholars will work with qualified advisors, and the format of the entire series will be coordinated by a major publishing house. Christian scholars on major secular university campuses, as well as some from the evangelical colleges, are participating. The reading target will be the American university student.

Q. What advice would you have for a layperson who is not an academic, but who wants to stay alert to ideas?

A. Don't get caught up in the experience-centered material of the day. The publishers are caught up in all this "I was into drugs; I was into this and that." That is simply repetitious. Follow the lists of the best books of the year in *Eternity* and other magazines, and see which ones are for you. Put C.S. Lewis high on your list. Work through Schaeffer and after you've worked through him, get into Henry and others. Remember who those men are who have contributed to the intellectual frontiers during the past generations: Gordon Clark, E.J. Carnell, and many others who've really made a contribution; their books are still worth reading. Get into a stimulating Sunday school class, where ideas are at the center of the class.

One thing my wife, Helga, and I have tried to do is to capture our social engagements for serious conversation. We belong to a neighborhood Bible study group, and also when we entertain for dinner we always have a group that is compatible and that will provide some intellectual stimulation. (*Eternity*, November 1980.)

For almost half a century since Carl F.H. Henry found Christ as a Long Island newspaperman he has contributed significantly to evangelical life and thought. Holder of five earned degrees—including doctorates in theology and philosophy—and numerous honorary degrees, he has taught on the faculties of leading evangelical seminaries and colleges. Currently, as lecturer at large for World Vision International, he teaches abroad annually for three months and has lectured to students on all the continents. His major theological work, *God, Revelation and Authority*, is in its third English printing, is available in Korean and Mandarin, and is being translated into German. Founding editor of *Christianity Today* from 1956-68, he was chairman of the 1966 World Congress of Evangelism in Berlin and the 1971 Jerusalem Conference on Biblical Prophecy. He is president of the American Theological Society and former president of the Evangelical Theological Society. His contributions to evangelical thought and life have had a shaping influence in theology, personal and social ethics, evangelism, and socio-political involvement. Henry currently lives in Arlington, Virginia, where with his wife Helga he maintains at 68 a disciplined work schedule that would stagger even many younger scholars. Because of Dr. Henry's unique contributions to the cause of evangelicalism, the editors of *Christianity Today* conducted this wide-ranging interview with him, to gather his insights and observations on a host of relevant theological, social, political, and ethical issues of the day.

Concerns and Considerations

Q. What religious trends do you consider most important?

Dr. Henry. The inability of political atheism (either behind the Iron Curtain or the Bamboo Curtain) to eradicate the religious nature of man; religion is flourishing under some governments officially committed to atheism.

The fascination that the experiential religion of the so-called electronic church holds for television viewers.

The continuing deterioration of the older liberal theology and its evident drift toward secular humanism.

The vulnerability to attack and negation of conventional ethics wedded to naturalistic metaphysics.

The failure of "process theology" to establish itself as a credible Christian option, thus revealing its nature as a philosophy of the university classroom, but not a religion of the people.

The intellectual probing and spiritual searching by university students, and their growing interest in the rational defense of evangelical theism.

The ongoing theological change among the evangelicals who compromise the full authority of Scripture and who, not surprisingly, find it increasingly difficult to maintain "all of orthodoxy except inerrancy."

Q. What do you foresee as key issues for the 1980's?

A. The problem of biblical authority will probably continue to disturb evangelicals very deeply. The issue will focus not simply on inerrancy, but also on interpretation as well, and especially on the culture-relatedness and culture-dependence of biblical revelation. Evangelicals insist that although the Bible was written in particular historical and cultural milieus, it speaks with binding authority to our different historical and cultural situations (for instance, on such a subject as marital faithfulness).

Another issue, resurfacing after lying quiescent for half a century, is higher criticism. Some evangelicals contend that conservative theological positions are compatible with liberal conclusions in "higher" or literary criticism of the Bible. But divergent, conflicting, and widening concessions will eventually show how deeply those mediating judgments are rooted in personal voluntary preferences rather than in rationally necessary conclusions.

There is also a growing danger that evangelicals may divide over political commitments.

Another key issue will be the problem of ecumenism. For nonevangelicals it will reemerge through an attempted rehabilitation of COCU (Consultation on Church Union). This may force institutions like Fuller Seminary to consider closer ecumenical identification. On the other hand, discontented evangelicals in theologically pluralistic mainline denominations will more seriously consider broader evangelical liaison either with consistent evangelicals from other mainline denominations or with evangelicals in the newer and (usually) smaller denominations committed as denominations to evangelical positions. Both evangelical and nonevangelical crosswinds are currently too confusing, however, to give a clear signal about any ecclesiastical realignment.

Q. Both you and Harold Lindsell hold to inerrancy. How would you distinguish your position from his?

A. In the successive stages of his "battle" for the Bible, Dr. Lindsell seems to be continually refining his views, and gratifyingly so. There were initially extreme positions: unjustifiably branding some evangelicals as "false," imposing the "domino theory" of inevitable apostasy on individuals, and so on. I still object to Lindsell's elevation of inerrancy over authority and inspiration as the *first* claim to be made for the Bible. His view of inerrancy also eclipses the equally important issues of revelation and culture, hermeneutics, and propositional revelation. To concentrate on inerrancy as the sole decisive issue is to wage the battle on too narrow a front. And I do not like the distrust he raises over all but a small handful of conservative institutions.

His overstatements made it easy for opponents of inerrancy to gain an undeserved sympathy for their views; such overstatements weakened the intellectual effectiveness of the evangelical thrust, and they cloaked the inerrancy forces with a reactionary image they do not deserve. One costly consequence was that evangelical enterprises like *Christianity Today* recoiled from aggressive involvement in a conflict in which the leading evangelical magazines might well have provided truly balanced leadership.

Q. What strategy would you urge to strengthen the churches' commitment to inerrancy?

A. The eye of the storm is shifting to two issues: the cultural conditioning of revelation, and the interpretation of Scripture. These central concerns bear on the possibility of our knowing and thus profiting from the truth. The churches should continue the Pauline stress on God's inspiration (really outbreathing) in order to *profit* man; our profit-oriented society strangely neglects the second half of II Timothy 3:16 with its emphasis on the profit of inspiration both intellectually and experientially.

As part of the church's educational program the crucial issues in debate should be freely discussed at the various levels of intellectual competence represented in the congregations. Church libraries need monographs of solid in-depth scholarship, and literature in a more popular vein. The aims in either case should be both theoretical and practical, issuing in a scriptural world-and-life view. Our writing should help clarify the Christian's role in society amid the vigorously presented alternatives. The goal should include a new devotion to personal and group Bible study. The Sunday school must become such an effective place to search Scripture that students change their minds and their lives.

Q. The idea of "propositional" revelation often comes under popular attack. Some say it suggests a God who reveals himself in Euclidian terms more appropriate for classroom debate than suited to the needs of real life. What do you mean when you affirm propositional revelation?

A. Simply that God reveals himself in intelligently formed statements. Nobody has ever caricatured Jesus as Euclidian because he spoke divine truths in human language. For instance, after telling the parable of the woman who found her lost coin, he said, "In the same way, I tell you, there is rejoicing in the presence of the angels of God over one sinner who repents" (Luke 15:10). The only connection between Euclid's geometry and the biblical idea of propositional revelation that I detect is that, like every logically formed system of doctrine, Euclid's geometry is built on axioms, or fundamental presuppositions, and that Christianity, too, has its basic "axioms" (the living God and intelligible divine revelation of truth) on which all its other claims depend. A God preoccupied with geometric abstractions is not my god; some say he was Galileo's. Evangelical Christians do not invite the world to an unknown and unknowable X!

A proposition is simply an intelligible, logically formed statement, a declarative sentence that is either true or false. The question is: Does God tell the truth or doesn't he? The evangelical maintains that he does. He asserts that Jesus spoke an understandable true statement when he said to the Jews, "... if you do not believe that I am the one I claim to be, you will indeed die in your sins" (John 8:24). To be sure, God reveals himself universally in nature, history, conscience, and the mind of man. But he reveals himself specially in Jesus Christ as attested by the Bible. While biblical revelation includes many commands and exhortations, it also provides at its very center true ideas about God and his relations to man and the world. We believe these biblical ideas are not just human guesses but verities that God has provided for us and the world.

The alternatives to propositional revelation are either that God gives us in the Bible only unsharable gobbledygook or that the Bible is just a book of human guesses, containing no revealed truths at all. Neo-orthodoxy teaches that divine revelation is not propositional; it denies that God reveals truths about himself and his purposes. Small wonder that this God concept collapses into existential decision and finally death-of-God speculation.

Q. Do you equate propositional revelation with the propositions or statements of the Bible?

A. By propositional revelation I mean not simply that the Bible is written in meaningful sentences—as most books are—but that God has revealed himself intelligibly and rationally in units of human speech involving sentences, words, and syntax that Scripture attests, and thus gives us an inspired literary document. Even when God revealed himself to the prophets in dreams and visions, the center of the revelation was always the shareable Word that the prophets prefaced by the formula: "Thus said the Lord . . ." God's universal revelation in nature and history, no less than his revelation in redemptive history, is an intelligible revelation. But for man fallen into sin, the content of that general revelation is objectively stated, along with the content of God's special saving revelation, in the truths set forth by the Bible.

Q. In your recent debate with Professor Daane of Fuller Theological Seminary, most of us agreed that Daane in the *Reformed Journal* seemed to give up the case for revealed truths. But some felt that you were uneasy with revelation that is personal. Would you care to comment?

A. Of course revelation is personal: its source is a personal God; it is addressed to persons; special revelation is often conveyed through persons, and supremely in the person of Jesus Christ. What I criticize is his Barthian insistence on "personal nonpropositional" revelation. Neo-orthodoxy rejects any objective divine revelation of truths to chosen prophets and apostles and now objectively given in Scripture. But the God of the Bible is not a dumb mute. He not only acts in external history but also intelligibly interprets his acts. Neo-orthodox theologians emphasize divine personal internal revelation intending thereby to reinforce the reality of God. But God who cannot be known to be "there" in any objective sense, soon simply fades into nothingness, like Lewis Carroll's Cheshire cat.

Q. Some reviewers call you a rationalist. Is that fair to your view?

A. If they are pleading the cause of irrationalism they are welcome to it. Christianity is a faith—but so are Buddhism, Shamanism, communism, and humanism. The main issue for the intellectual world is whether the biblical revelation is credible; that is, are there good reasons for believing it? I am against the paradox mongers and those who emphasize only personal volition and decision. They tell us we are to believe even in the absence of good reasons for believing. Some even argue that to seek to give reasons for the faith within us is a sign of lack of trust or an exercise in self-justification. This is nonsense. Against any view that faith is merely a leap in the dark, I insist on the reasonableness of Christian faith and the "rationality" of the living, self-revealed God. I maintain that God creates and preserves the universe through the agency of the Logos, that man by creation bears the moral and rational (as opposed to irrational) image of his Maker, that despite the fall, man is still responsible for knowing God. I believe that divine revelation is rational, that the inspired biblical canon is a consistent and coherent whole, that genuine faith seeks understanding, that the Holy Spirit uses truth as a means of persuasion, that logical consistency is a test of truth, and that saving trust in Christ necessarily involves acceptance of certain revealed propositions about him. We are called to "reasonable service" (Rom. 12:1) of the Logos and, further, that nurturing "the Christian mind" is a crucial aspect of spiritual growth. Those who reject these affirmations rest their case on neo-Protestant and neo-Christian novelties rather than on historic evangelical and biblical theism.

Q. What ethical developments are noteworthy?

A. First, fierce moral relativity is encompassing our secular society. Having lost its biblical moorings, our age stifles its conscience and displays an utterly shameless sensuality. One cannot but note the rampant perversion of sex, the breakdown of family life, and the cruelty and inhumanity evident in the ready massacre of fetal life. One must mention also the failure of the great universities to sustain fixed moral values, the inability of humanism to mount ethical resources requiring self-sacrifice, and the widening effort by frontier scientists to gloss over the ethical and moral implications of their experiments by an appeal to mere utilitarianism. Then too, prime-time television highlights cultural trivialities and poses little challenge to ethical waywardness. Yet I detect a new longing by disenchanted youth—after a spate of sinful living—for personal worth and for lasting love. Some are turning to the life-changing dynamic that revealed religion offers even the most profligate.

Q. Do you see the Bible as having significance for public issues?

Concerns and Considerations 87

A. The Bible lays an authoritative claim upon both our generation and all nations. Neither the protests of radical biblical critics nor those of secular humanists have invalidated that claim. Neglect of the main elements of biblical revelation renders most modern intellectual centers powerless. It may seem trite, and I know it leaves unsettled the matter of political specifics, but nothing is more needed than national repentance—national repentance on the part of people ungrateful for their blessings, and unwilling to make the moral sacrifices requisite for national well-being. The times cry out for spiritual renewal alive to the high claims of divine truth and universal morality, for ethical dedication to neighborly good will, to human rights and duties under God. A nation that settles its political specifics in this context cannot go far wrong, and even when it does, it has a built-in method of correcting its mistakes. The illusion that all the world's problems can be solved merely by political change is disastrous. But to neglect political imperatives can likewise be naturally devastating.

Q. How do you regard the alleged growth of the evangelical movement?

A. "The more, the better" makes nonsense if there is confusion about who evangelicals are. Traditional evangelical agencies seem no longer to preserve the term "evangelical" for the biblical essentials. The term is becoming a banner over many aberrations, and it increasingly means different things to different people. Some revel in "the day of the evangelical" and, to show how multitudinous the army is, boast of all possible varieties. Others define the term too narrowly and propose a purge list of "false evangelicals," thus pitting brother against brother in the body of Christ. Still others, pleading evangelistic priorities or denominational peace, avoid or even repress open discussion of the inerrancy of Scripture.

Q. Do you think it is possible for the NAE to become an effective counterweight to the NCC?

A. Given a coalescsence of the right leadership, the right issues, the right program, the right strategy, and the right launch pad, NAE could still attract wide grassroots support. But many evangelicals now look upon it as almost as irrelevant as the United Nations. NAE has played too small a part in accelerating a cooperative evangelistic thrust, in coping with the evangelical authority crisis, in launching evangelicals into today's cultural and political crisis. It has not effectively coordinated fellow evangelicals in the mainline ecumenical churches. For all that, NAE is to be commended for its many constructive activities.

Q. How do you assess the awakening evangelical interest in politics?

A. Evangelicals must get their priorities straight. Christians have a biblical mandate to preach the gospel to the world and to work for national righteousness. I'm gratified that evangelicals are finding their way back into the public arena, but disconcerted lest they act unwisely and lose their opportunity. The strident criticisms by liberal intellectuals need not trouble us; evangelicals are damned for social lethargy if they are not involved, and damned for intruding sectarianism into politics if they oppose cherished prejudices. It does, I think, reflect adversely upon evangelicals when many show less interest in getting biblical truth and right into national life than in promoting a born-again candidate or in getting prayer back into the public schools. The evangelical movement needs to get publicly involved for the sake of social justice, not simply for the sake of private moral renewal.

Evangelicals tend to be single-issue or single-candidate oriented. Their agenda is often much narrower than that of Catholics, ecumenists, and liberal Jews. However, the ecumenists, who have long championed special causes, are in no position to protest. They have criticized single-issue involvement (for example, prolife, though sure not ERA!), and have conveniently and routinely overlooked some specific moral issues, like inflation, crime, alcoholism, and addiction to cigarettes and drugs. They have baptized Communist rulers in Hanoi and Peking and Havana as revolutionary carriers of divine justice.

Q. What should evangelicals do?

A. They had better agree on an agenda, make their objectives known, and move toward a better day. The American economy and foreign policy are in disarray and the moral temper of the nation is low. All citizens have public duties and are called to support the right and the good in national life. Yet the Christian fails his nation if he permits the evangelistic imperative to eclipse political duty. Evangelical churches need to speak out on both the gospel of grace and the revealed principles of social and political life.

This must be done without confusing specifics valid only for the Hebrew theocracy with civic imperatives for pluralistic nations envisioned in the New Testament. Instead of seeking political power, the churches should delineate and promote the proper use of power. God's people should be a mighty voice for justice in the land—aware that biblical justice does not necessarily coincide with propagandistic perceptions of justice. Given a comprehensive vision and theology of politics illumined by scriptural principles, God's people have the task of translating these into policies and platforms and support for desirable programs and candidates.

Q. What of a Christian or evangelical party?

A. To take the route of a Christian party is, in my view, a mistake. But neither is it right to commit oneself unreservedly to one of the existing parties. Better yet, why not forge a moral majority in which evangelicals join forces locally with their townspeople on crucial issues? This would overcome the specter of an ecclesiastical party. Participation in local politics is good training for state and national involvement; the opportunity for political engagement in the United States is exceptional, a privilege unknown in many modern nations. The Christian ought to be politically active to the limit of his or her opportunity and competence. Unfortunately, these two qualifications do not always coincide. The Christian should try to bring into the political arena objectivity and balance, and especially, concern for the general welfare rather than personal self-interest.

Q. What do you think of the direct role taken by prominent evangelical preachers in political campaigning?

A. The clergy are ordained to preach the Word of God and should "stick to their last," that of clarifying the truth of revelation, including the Judeo-Christian principles of personal and social ethics, and of exhorting church members to exemplify and apply those principles as conscientiously and consistently as possible in public affairs.

Q. What is your reaction to the identification of evangelicals with the new political right?

A. If political pluralism means anything, then evangelical Christians have as much right to promote their views as anybody else. But the Moral Majority has claimed to be not a minority but a block of 30 million votes that could decisively affect national outcomes. The secular press recognized that as an exaggeration. The Bible gives no blueprint for a universal evangelical political order. The Moral Majority was misguided by its leaders, who promoted a Christian litmus test of specific issues used to approve or disapprove particular candidates. Its spokesmen retreated to an espousal of "principles" without carefully defining them or logically deriving specifics from them.

The evangelical right differs in significant ways from the intellectual, political right. The evangelical right lacks historical perspective, theological depth, and philosophical rationale (most would be astonished to learn that classical political liberalism first promoted some positions that political conservatism now champions). It seeks a quick fix and misunderstands the historical depth of sinful perversity. Corrupt features of a society often have resulted from deeply entrenched wickedness that only a change of mind and will can alter. Effective social change requires both a political and a spiritual thrust. Shallowness accommodates a promotion of right-wing causes simply as political and economic preferences rather than on principle and by reasoned argument. Moral Majority was reluctant to dissociate itself from the campaigns of some political conservatives, including a criminally convicted (Abscam) legislator and another congressman involved in a repulsive sexual offense. In a simplistic way, moreover, the conservative litmus test leveled to the same plane of black or white, very different kinds of issues, such as abortion and the B-1 bomber. The consistent alternative to the political left, which all too often follows a pragmatic more than a principled course, is an informed and self-critical right.

Q. Do you have any warning to evangelicals standing on the left wing of political and social involvement?

A. They run the risk of turning into an illusory ideology what often begins as a proper protest against a simplistic conservative solution. Socialism has failed woefully to live up to its promises, and communism even more so; the notion that they are benevolent is ill-founded. Why duplicate the errors of the ecumenical left? Pragmatically oriented programs too often end up in glaring contradictions, such as promoting American pacifism while approving the violence and revolution of others. The whole Christian heritage stands on the side of peaceful, legal, and orderly processes of change in society, rather than on the side of violence and revolution.

Q. How influential are the mass media?

A. The average American gives 15 percent of his time to the mass media and less than one percent to the church. The emergence of the electronic church indicates that many people hunger for a personal faith. Much of this programming encourages an experiential religion, which, however, in the absence of adequate biblical teaching, can lead to theological error. The Christian movement must use the media to confront people's basic assumptions, habits, and even subconscious drives, by sharing the truth of God's revelation. Instead of allowing the media to crowd out the Mediator, the claim of the Mediator must be affirmed upon and through the media.

Q. What practical steps could evangelicals take to achieve their objectives in public life?

A. 1. *In the local churches:* repent and rededicate ourselves to the service of God; reject the proud pretense that evangelical politicians or even an evangelical majority can right the wrongs of the nation and perhaps of the world; clarify the relation and difference between the political and the evangelistic duty of Christians, lest misguided congregations proclaim: "Behold the candidate who solves all the problems of the nation," and neglect the message: "Behold the Lamb of God who takes away the sin of the world."

2. *Among the leaders:* share convictions, identify national goals, and explore common and divergent strategies for achieving them; links with nonevangelicals who share our political concerns and aims should also be on the agenda.

3. *In the thought journals and evangelical colleges and seminaries:* explore scriptural principles governing political life and divergent inferences drawn from biblical principles; encourage articles, theses, dissertations, and books; explore and weigh national priorities; mount a great wave of public opinion in which faculty and students share; and enlist evangelical and other media in the cause of national political renewal. (*Christianity Today*, March 13, 1981.)

Dr. Carl F.H. Henry, described by supporters as "dean of America's evangelical theologians," will discuss "The Evangelical Prospect in America" July 11 during an 8 a.m. breakfast gathering at Sacramento's First Baptist Church. He is founding editor of *Christianity Today*, the country's foremost evangelical journal, which marks its 25th anniversary in the July 17 issue.

Henry was a kind of "voice crying in the wilderness," the proponent of evangelical respectability, during the 1950s and 1960s when what he calls "the ecumenical churches" appeared to be the mainstream of American Protestant thought. Many credit him with providing the intellectual underpinnings for what in the 1980s has become the Evangelical Movement.

Henry, now semi-retired, currently is lecturer-at-large for World Vision International. *Bee* staff writer Robin Witt caught up with Henry at Berkeley's New College where he is teaching this summer. Here is part of that interview.

Evangelicals' Influence Continues Its Upsurge

Q. What is the prospect for evangelicals in America?
Dr. Henry. I think the evangelical upsurge is still under way, and there are a lot of explanations which miss the mark. Some people try to dismiss it in terms of conservative politics or others say it fulfills an emotional need. But I think the evangelicals are on the brink of the most spectacular penetration of American life and thought in this century.

I'm not sure they are fully going to capitalize on it. I think there is some danger of dissipating it through internal conflict and maybe uncoordinated strategy and maybe limited goals, narrow goals.

Q. Is there an "evangelical awakening" occurring in America?
A. I think it's premature to say (America) is going through an evangelical awakening. I think that the real test of an evangelical awakening is when public conscience judges itself by biblical criteria, even though it may not be personally committed. And I don't think we've seen that yet.

Q. You have written that the evangelicals may not be as strong as they think they are—only that "ecumenical churches" and "secular humanism" are in disarray. How strong is the movement?
A. Well, I certainly think it has the initiative on the American scene. And I think it is growing. Not all churches are growing, but the ones that are growing are the evangelical churches.

And it certainly has come out of the closet and into the public arena. I think that's a great gain, whatever the risks and whatever the vulnerability. I think at least it's broken out of its withdrawal from public life and the political arena.

Q. What will be their impact in politics?
A. I don't see an evangelical political party on the horizon and I think that's good. But I do see an evangelical coalition on many points of agreement. I think moral absolutes are relevant

to public life and not simply to private affairs. And any nation which ignores moral absolutes is in danger of marching off the map.

But I think the evangelicals need to give a good deal of thought to the question of what absolutes ought to be legislated and on what basis.

Q. Has America ever used a strictly biblical morality in governing itself?

A. America is not a theocracy in the way that the ancient Hebrew nation was a theocracy. When evangelicals speak of returning America to its moorings as a Christian nation, I think they run the risk of misinterpreting America as if it were a covenant nation akin to the Hebrew theocracy.

Christians on this side of the New Testament live under a pluralistic pattern of government and they are scattered worldwide under all patterns of government.

I think there's a difference between a Christian nation—that is, the people and their regard for a claim of moral absolutes upon all of life—and a Christian government.

The Moral Majority sometimes is ambiguous as to whether it wants to legislate what the Bible teaches or whether it wants to legislate on the grounds of revealed religion.

Q. How then do we define morality in a pluralistic and democratic society?

A. To be sure the will of the majority is significant and that's one thing that the Moral Majority has emphasized—the majority of people in the United States are not interested in a morality with an increasing permissiveness and without norms.

They are much more on the side of coventional morality. They want laws that reflect that. I would say a Christian, or a Jewish or a humanistic minority are on equal grounds. If the Christian majority doesn't promote its positions, it will be deluged by some other majority.

So yes, I would say the will of the majority is what counts in a democracy. But the Christian would want to be self-assured that the principles for which he or she stands are not simply a reflection of the majority, but also reflect the will of God.

Q. Couldn't the Evangelical Movement be an expression of cultural popularity, much as the Protestant Mainline churches

—what you call "ecumenical churches"—were a generation ago? And couldn't it die just as quickly?

A. I think that what really accounts for the emergence of the evangelicals is, first, that they are evangelistic. And a movement that doesn't do evangelism, and doesn't reproduce itself, soon dies.

And, secondly, they are unapologetically supernaturalistic. And those who said that God has had His day really misunderstand human nature and they oversimplify reality.

And then the evangelicals have a sense of moral authority and of life-transforming power. There are stories like (President Nixon's special counsel) "Chuck" Colson, of his coming through Watergate and then a felon (who emerged as) a sort of modern apostle to the imprisoned.

And then there is a doctrinal stability. They aren't always modifying their doctrines . . . I think those are the factors that really explain the emergence of the evangelicals, rather than sociological considerations.

Q. What do you mean by "ecumenical churches"?

A. I mean that effort by 20th century Christianity that sought one world church predicated on theological inclusiveness.

Q. You have often questioned whether they can survive into the 21st century. Can they?

A. Some of them are in real trouble. Some of the denominations are much more open to an evangelical ingredient. You take the Presbyterian denomination. You have the loss of many churches. The churches that are growing are the evangelical churches.

And some of the biggest churches are known first as evangelical churches and only second as denominational. That in itself tells a story. And the ecumenical seminaries are a shambles, theologically.

Q. Can these "ecumenical churches" renew themselves?

A. I would say the neglect of evangelistic and spiritual concerns in the interest of political affairs was one factor (in the eclipse of "ecumenical churches"). And especially there was the activity of the political left, the funding of revolutionary causes.

Secondly, there was the failure to take theology seriously,

or doctrine seriously. This was reflected in the theological pluralism of the ecumenical movement in which one found the whole spectrum of belief, from the right to the radicals of the left who denied the miracles and the reality of the supernatural and the divinity of Christ. (*The Sacramento Bee*, July 4, 1981.)

This summer, Denver was one of the stop-over points in Dr. Henry's lecture circuit. During his one-week stay to teach at Conservative Baptist Theological Seminary, Dr. Henry talked with *His People* about his perceptions of evangelical Christianity, secular humanism, democracy and education.

Humanism, Christianity Will Clash

Q. Dr. Henry, is humanism the strongest influence in public education?

Dr. Henry. Secular humanism certainly does not represent, I'm convinced, even a majority of the university professors. But it is what someone has called a "hidden curriculum of public education"—not by any official action by the establishment, but by the pervasive influence that it aggrandizes to itself. For that, we are to blame because we do not effectively challenge it.

The evangelicals work around it and they press their claims for the supernatural outside the classroom... Now it's the radical students who more and more challenge the combination of raw naturalism with ethical imperatives, a plea for social justice and racial equality. It's the radicals—the leftist students—who are saying more and more to the professors, "we share your naturalism but we don't see how you get your ethics out of it."

Q. Do you see a greater role for Christian education as a separate system, or do Christians need to take a deep breath and dive into the secular system to redeem or change it?

A. We need to restore the educational system to a quest for the *whole* truth. We need to go in both directions. There is no principial necessity for separate Christian schools—only a strategic necessity at times. That necessity arises when the tide of secular education is so biased that it overwhelmingly erodes the convictions of the younger generation.

At that time there is a strategic necessity for Christian schools—in order to train up a vanguard to challenge those alternatives effectively—to unmask them and to present the alternatives in a compelling way. But many of our evangelical institutions are like sheltered nurseries that are not concerned with transplanting their cuttings into the larger world of nature.

Q. Some observers say that secular humanism is on the rise. Others say it is declining. Which view is true?

A. Which way it's going or where it will be in five or ten years is not given in the inevitabilities of history. The way history goes depends in large measure on what we do with it. I think the Moral Majority has already made a significant difference in mood, attitude and probably in the courage of a lot of people . . . and to some less extent, significant political change in where we're going.

Even if secular humanism is not on the rise, it has a grip today on the shaping centers of contemporary life. It is reflected in the stance of many in the legal and judicial establishment. It certainly has its grip on the political order.

Before the advent of the Moral Majority or Right to Life Movement, there was a tendency to cater to the concessive minority as if democratic pluralism required a tolerance for immorality without any moral absolutes. That increasingly pervaded the political arena. It's only now—since the polls show that position may jeopardize their future—that politicians are starting to run for cover. Whether that means a basic change of political outlook or not, is another question—or whether they're just statistically oriented.

You have not only the legal order and the political order, but the educational arena. The educational establishment wants to push creation wholly beyond mention while evolution is taught as a necessary part of the academic curriculum.

Then there is the pervasive influence of the mass media. There is little question that there is more integrity among journalists than some radical critics give them credit for. But I do think it's fair to say that representatives of the press are not at home in a discussion of moral absolutes and they find just the discussion of moral absolutes enigmatic.

Q. Will we see a major confrontation between humanists and Christians?

A. It is only now, in the last few years, that the shaping forces of American life are not one-sidedly secular humanist, but that there are two forces that have now emerged and are on a collision course. One of them is the approval and promulgation of secular humanism through formative institutions. The other is a grass roots revival of dedication to the conventional biblical values. This is reflected in the growth of the evangelical churches, and secondly, reflected in the growth of the Christian day school movement across the country. We see the rise of the electronic church where conventional values are emphasized along with the evangel. We see the rise of the political right—the evangelical political right.

Both of these movements (humanism and evangelicalism) have gone far already. The humanists are regrouping and intensifying their positions. The evangelical forces on the other side are beginning to shape an effective coalition.

I don't see any possibility for a Christian political party. That would be a tragedy. But I do think we can see possibilities for evangelical coalition. And that means with non-evangelicals as well for certain matters, because the morally sensitive people of this country are not totally evangelical. And some evangelicals have been too insensitive to social concerns, as we well know.

Q. What are the biggest problems for humanists and evangelicals?

A. There are two things to be said about both of these movements which are now on a collision course. Each of them carries within itself a certain ambiguity with which it must cope.

For the humanists, the question is how to derive its emphasis on the universal and permanent dignity of man out of a merely evolutionary philosophy. How do you get ethics out of raw naturalism—that's its dilemma.

The evangelicals have a certain ambiguity. For them the complex maneuver is how to merge legality and morality—the legislation of morals in a pluralistic society. That is their big issue.

Q. How do you see evangelicals' position in terms of law and justice?

A. Evangelicals right now are very vulnerable. By throwing the weight of evangelical impact on an appeal to the majority—by emphasizing that lawyers and judges and scientists and journalists are really out of step with the majority and their attitudes toward immorality—evangelicals tend to encourage a *sociological* referrent—rather than a *biblical* one—for the decisions between right and wrong.

The real answer is that God has revealed himself and made himself known. The fact that some people don't believe it doesn't discredit it for others—doesn't invalidate it for others. People are free to be pagans if they want to be, but why should they impose that on the rest of society? (*His People*, August, 1981.)

Interview by *Light* magazine, publication of the Christian Life Commission of the Southern Baptist Convention.

Christians in Politics

Q. You have said that "spiritual rebirth bestows no special competence for resolving political specifics, although it should assure a high level of moral integrity." What do Christians have to contribute to the political process?

Dr. Henry. Much every way. First, by clarifying to the world who is truly the Lord, King, Führer of the universe, and by calling mankind above all else to knowing and doing God's revealed will. This Christians do best through the church's vital existence in the world as the New Society ruled by the crucified and risen Jesus—a body of humanity that insists upon obeying God above man. In a fallen society, God wills the church for certain objectives, through evangelism as a means, and civil government for other objectives, through legislation or coercion as the means. Civil government therefore has a *necessary* but *limited* function (against chaos and anarchy on the one hand and against totalitarian rule on the other). Christians should affirm that God is the source of justice and of universal human rights. They should no less affirm, but through voluntary evangelism as the means, that God is the fountain of mercy who provides a salvation without which all men are doomed in their iniquity, forgives the sins of the penitent, and gives a new power for righteousness. A just political order presupposes both a constitution as a relatively stable standard by which successive regimes or administrations are to be judged, and a transcendent standard of justice by which all constitutions are judged. Christians should promote respect for law, therefore, without promoting an idolatry of law. They should be on the side of government and law and order as the ideal framework through which God seeks to promote earthly justice and peace in a fallen, pluralistic society. Christians should pray for rulers and for national righteousness, be exemplary citizens, promote justice in public affairs, and serve with integrity in public office as opportunity arises.

Q. Why is it important for Christians to be involved in politics?

A. If godly people do not become involved they will inevitably be ruled by the ungodly. Moreover, Christians are to support civil authority not only for expedience sake but for conscience sake (Rom. 13). They are to pray for (not against) rulers, and are to promote public righteousness. Justice, moreover, is not self-defining; Christians can illumine the debate over the public order in terms of imperatives enunciated by the biblically-revealed God of justice.

Q. How relevant is the theocratic model of government seen in the Old Testament for Christians trying to exert an influence on American government?

A. America is not a covenant nation as was ancient Israel. Since New Testament times, God has willed the dispersion of believers throughout the politically pluralistic nations for the sake of world witness and service. The Old Testament reveals not only the universal principles of social ethics but also stipulates specific legislation for the theocracy. Some of that legislation may have value beyond the Old Testament, but not on a covenant-nation basis. The alternative to theocracy is not secular political relativism, unbridled self-interest, and military expansionism. America has had a providential role in modern history, and has been a source of blessing to many nations; presently her future is clouded.

Q. Is government in the New Testament more pluralistic than in the Old Testament? What insights do you draw from the New Testament to guide Christians?

A. In the sense that there are now more than 150 nations, the political arena is clearly more pluralistic; in New Testament times the Roman empire was the world power. God wills civil government but reveals no single preferred form. The millennium involves a beneficent monarchy. But since in a sinful society accumulated power invites corruption, democracy is preferable, for in principle the masses can then determine their own destiny. Yet democracy has been in retreat in this century as the shadow of totalitarian tyranny falls over the modern world and as it staggers under internal weaknesses, through its elevation of majority will over the will of God, and through the pressure of disparate minorities. Christians are called to live in many contexts. They should not be anti-government but rather pro-justice. Thus they topple governments only indirectly, as government places itself in the service of injustice, although civil disobedience has apostolic precedent when the state requires the church to do what God forbids.

Q. Tell *Light* readers what groups and individuals you associate with the term "New Religious Right." Which ones are the most important in 1982?

A. Moral Majority, Religious Roundtable, Christian Voice, and *Conservative Digest*. Moral Majority is probably most significant, though the number of financially supportive contributions is considerably less than the constituency numbers frequently bandied about.

Q. The influence of the New Religious Right on the 1980 presidential election is a widely discussed topic. Some have claimed it is responsible for Reagan's success. Jerry Falwell has said that the perception of that influence is much greater than the reality. How important do you think the New Religious Right was in Reagan's success?

A. It was clearly a factor in the election of Ronald Reagan. It counted *doubly* because of a conservative, evangelical defection from President Carter and an aggressive switch to candidate Reagan.

Q. A frequent criticism of the New Religious Right is a strong tendency in the direction of single-issue politics. Is this a valid criticism? Is a comprehensive political program necessary?

A. Sometimes single issues are of immense importance; that can be said of the abortion issue, for example, although even that issue might better have been perceived as part of a cluster of issues bearing on preservation of the family as the basic unit of society. A comprehensive political philosophy is even more imperative than a comprehensive program. The slaughter of a million fetuses a year, mostly in the interest of birth control, is a horrendous outbreak of pagan immorality. But the political left, it should be noted, has been as prone as the political right to promote single issues.

Q. What do Christians getting involved in politics need to learn?

A. That political candidates even for the presidency now run on one platform and after election, readily forget their promises; that effective political involvement begins at the precinct level; that the providence of God is a neglected factor in political considerations; that the paucity of leadership may reflect the judgment of God; that biblical principles sometimes accommodate a variety of inferences; that statute law is fashioned in an arena of political compromise and is vulnerable to revision; that political engagement is not a matter of bringing in the kingdom of God; that Christians ought nonetheless to be politically active to the limit of their competence and ability.

Q. Is secular humanism as much of a consistent philosophy as some of the religious critics of public schools say it is? Are the public schools really inculcating a "religion"?

A. The public schools by and large engender the notion that religion is irrelevant. Many teachers are not secular humanists; some are devout Christians. But the philosophy that more influentially than any other gets through the classroom today is secular humanism: the reduction of reality to space-time processes and events, the transiency of all existence, the relativity of all ideas and ideals to their cultural setting, and man as the definer of truth and the good. To be sure, the university world has gone anti-intellectual at the student level. Students embrace humanism less as an intellectual commitment than they do as an excuse for defecting from the inherited religion of the West. But many professors are astounded because despite the classroom orientation thousands of students, despite the humanistic mind-set, have become evangelical believers. My guess would be that on balance the secular universities more effectively communicate humanism than many of our religious colleges succeed in communicating biblical theism. Many humanists, incidentally, are not reluctant to regard humanism as a religion.

Q. Senator Helms has said that he would regard as voluntary prayer a teacher writing the words to a Catholic prayer on the board and asking the students to join the teacher in reciting those words. Do you agree?

A. If they join voluntarily I suppose it is voluntary. But prayer won't help matters much if it becomes a Jewish prayer on Monday, a Catholic prayer on Tuesday, a Lutheran prayer on Wednesday, a Southern Baptist prayer on Thursday, a humanistic prayer on Friday, or if it becomes a least-common denominator alternative through the week, or no prayer on Sunday or at midweek prayer meeting. There should be opportunity for voluntary prayer, but not officially-stipulated prayers.

Q. Why does the New Religious Right have such a strong pro-Israel emphasis? Do you see any dangers in it?

A. It considers the return of Jewry to Palestine a fulfillment of biblical prophecy, sees Israel as the one sure bulwark against Soviet expansion in the Near East, and emphasizes that the Bible promises blessing to those who befriend God's covenant-people. The dangers are clear. Some New Right statements are less critical of Israeli policy than of American policy. While Jewry could hardly survive in Palestine unless Israel survives, what is forgotten is that God will judge the injustices of Israel no less than those of any other nation, that the provocations between Israel and her Arab neighbor nations continue to invite a horrendous confrontation, and that the failure of the Jew to recognize Jesus as Messiah is from the New Testament standpoint a matter of culpable blindness.

Q. Jerry Falwell identifies a pro-Israel emphasis as a part of the pro-America agenda for Moral Majority. Yet he says that the Moral Majority is strictly political and not religious. Do you think these claims are consistent?

A. Jerry Falwell wears numerous hats and it is often unclear which one he has just put on. He has modified some positions, however, when implications and inconsistencies are clarified. Instead of putting fellow evangelicals on a "hit list" over their isolated or objectionable differences from ours, we ought first to probe areas of mutual agreement, concentrate on commonalities, and put differences in this larger perspective.

Q. Do you see this pro-Israel emphasis and eschatological views as reasons for support of President Reagan's current military buildup?

A. Possibly. But the big factor is the expansionism of the predator powers—the Soviets and Afghanistan, Cuba, and so on. The United States should in the present world condition be second to no power militarily. But massive military budgets place an immense burden on modern nations; they continually damage themselves and provoke each other by this endless escalation. A bilateral halt in the arms race involving on-site verification should be an international objective.

Q. Is the current military buildup moving us closer to war or peace?

A. Who but God knows? But if to war, we had best be ready. The cost of not being prepared will be higher than the cost of being prepared. The Eastern European peoples are paying an almost unbelievably high price for their totalitarian subjection; read Solzhenitsyn's *Gulag Archipelago*.

Q. Jerry Falwell, with his strong pro-Israel perspective, argued against the AWACS sale. Billy Graham, who has identified working for peace as the second priority for his ministry (behind a continuation of his evangelistic preaching), apparently sought to counter this strong pro-Israel view in the Senate vote. How do these two major Christian voices arrive at such different conclusions?

A. The question seems somewhat loaded. Billy Graham is not for unilateral disarmament; Jerry Falwell thinks the AWACS sale works against stability and peace. It's best to let them explain their reasons firsthand, rather than to run the risk of misjudging motivations and intentions. I suspect that neither Graham, Falwell, Henry nor Foy Valentine has infallibility in this area, and I know of no verse even in the Amplified Bible that settles the matter.

Q. Why do you think the New Religious Right has so strongly identified with conservative fiscal policy?

A. Because unless a sound monetary policy is achieved, America will go down the drain economically and the other nations with it. Inflation is a moral issue. A sound dollar is one of the best ways to help the unemployed, the poor, the elderly, the working class, and the nation as a whole.

Q. Do you think the emphasis upon voluntarism, charity, and the private sector is a realistic way of dealing with poverty and welfare?

A. It surely is the option that apostolic Christianity exercised in reaching out to needs of the household of faith and then beyond. It should say something significant to a nation and to the world that a godly people respond compassionately to the needs of the congregation. There should be a job corps in each of the Christian churches, concerned to probe work opportunities for unemployed members. To be sure, Christians have high motivations for reaching out beyond the household of faith to others in need: God made all humans in his image, and Christ died for sinners everywhere. But responding to destitution is not a duty of Christians only but of every man everywhere. The masses in the great centers of destitution—India, Pakistan, Bangladesh, Indonesia—are Muslims and Hindus. It is scandalous that petrol-rich Arab oil sheiks drop millions of dollars in a single night at the gaming tables in London, and that Hindu leaders oppose aid to the lowest caste as an attack on established religion, culture, and social stability. The government of India sells grain to Russia. Social action and evangelism are therefore both needed, to change human motivation and compassion. To be sure, government must be involved where voluntarism fails, but it should not be a first resort, and all governments would ideally be involved on some justly proportionate basis.

Q. It is obvious that Christians differ widely in what they think Christian involvement in politics means. How specific is the Bible in providing insights for Christians to follow? Does it have a word for us on issues like nuclear power, building missiles, and caring for the poor in our society?

A. The Bible gives us revealed principles of social ethics but few specifics for resolving the political dilemmas facing the twentieth century or any other. It leaves to successive generations the ways in which nations can best use their legitimate power to restrain injustice, preserve peace, and respond to needs of the poor. Nuclear power is no more evil than is matter (as some Greek philosophers thought); it is the use to which it is put that is decisive.

Q. The United States is a pluralistic society. American Christianity is quite diverse. What do you foresee for organized efforts at influencing the government of the United States? Should an attempt be made to establish a Christian party?

A. If there is a Christian party, the churches will inherit the blame for all political failures of that party. I see no likelihood at the moment of a national Christian party. But either American evangelicals will align themselves in coalition on certain political objectives that they share in common or there will be evangelical collapse, conflict, and chaos in their political stance, and the last state of their involvement will be worse than their earlier noninvolvement.

Q. Describe for *Light* readers some elements of a strategy you recommend for penetrating the political realm with Christian influence.

A. Christians should be the champions, first and foremost, of freedom, especially in an age of totalitarian tyranny. They should be perceived not simply as promoters of a particular political and religious agenda, but as champions of the rights of all humans under God, as advocates of liberty to act according to the will of God rather than submit to the arbitrary demands of rulers or even the preferences of a majority of fellow citizens. Christians should agree on certain national goals—I would put the stability of the family high on the list, and the issues of work and poverty, and war and peace—and chart their agreements and disagreements. They should not press upon a pluralistic society specifically theological reasons why citizens generally should support the views Christians advocate, except where government requires Christians to do what God forbids, or where government invites a statement of ecclesial positions, or where Christians have first joined others in a common public protest against protracted injustice and then mounted a supplementary witness to the God of justice and of justification. But it is through effective evangelistic preaching in a media age that the church has its great (and too much neglected) opportunity of preaching to the conscience of the nation, and of indicating the criteria by which Christ at his return will judge men and nations and is in fact currently judging them, and by which standards they ought therefore now to live. (*Light*, July-August 1982.)

Religious Broadcasting magazine interviews Carl F.H. Henry, featured speaker at the 40th anniversary banquet of the National Religious Broadcasters national convention in Washington, D.C., January 30-February 2, 1983.

Worldview of a Theologian

Whether politics or theology, all things find their ultimate meaning in God's Word

Q. As you approach age 70 what changes mark your outlook on life?

Dr. Henry. A Christian knows that he will not be engulfed by this earth and that the time approaches when one moves up from it. One thinks more often, in his travels, not simply that "I shall likely not see this city again" but rather that "I shall view this planet soon under wholly new conditions."

Q. Life was different when you were a lad?

A. In many parts of the world it remains primitive; wasn't it that way in Jesus' day? I hopscotched on the sidewalks of New York's East Side and then romped over a one-acre Long Island farm where we grew our own vegetables, plowed with a decrepit horse and raised some goats. In winter we braved the cold winds that swept beneath the grape arbor leading to the outhouse where an old Sears-Roebuck catalog transported us to different worlds. My father sank a 21-foot well and we carried water upstairs to a tub. It was a six-mile trip by bus to high school; we walked a mile to grade school and to Sunday school. Our home had a smoke-house in the cellar, and still in the kitchen, and was lit by kerosene wick lamps. I remember the arrival of a paved road, electric lights, and finally a telephone when I began work as a teenage reporter.

Q. What was the biggest thing that came into your life in those years?

A. God as a personal reality, overarching the opportunities of a newspaper career. Then followed a divine constraint to do what nobody in our family had done—pursue a college education. At Wheaton College I met Helga, a devout missionary daughter who needed to be persuaded that she ought not to marry any of the others already in line.

Helga was and remains a priceless treasure to me. She came to college from the Cameroon mission field where her parents pioneered. Surviving without a bank balance was nothing strange to her; for more than a week, unbeknown to anybody, she had lived on fruit fallen from trees along the route to campus.

Q. By the time you entered Wheaton College your horizons had shifted considerably beyond the simple early beginnings?
A. I was 22, had six solid years of Long Island journalistic training and experience. Already at the age of 20 I had edited a long-established weekly paper and was reporting for New York papers, covering political as well as other affairs. I worked my way through college as a suburban stringer for the *Chicago Daily Tribune, Wheaton Daily Journal* and other papers.

I still recall dragging into Latin class at eight in the morning from all night coverage of a double murder and suicide, to be greeted—when I hadn't prepared the lesson—by the professor's dispassionate recital of the principal parts of the verb *flunko* (her creation): *flunko, flunkere, faculty flunktus*! I taught some journalism at Wheaton and some typing also: in fact, in one of those typing classes I met my wife. She was more interested in typing than in either matrimony or me at the time.

Q. Your life has spanned World War I, World War II and the present international upheavals. What lessons from a biblical perspective would you draw from history?
A. The failure of efforts to achieve world unity and world peace through global military dominance and on the basis of human unregeneracy. The Bible affirms that the unity of human history lies in the moral and spiritual purpose of God who punishes sin and rewards righteousness.

Q. What do you think will be the status of the United States, Soviet Russia, mainland China and Israel at the end of this century?
A. Who can tell but God? Neither historical analysis nor political prediction can guarantee the future, which God controls. The Bible speaks of regathered Israel; there is no express

mention of America, Japan and other great modern powers.

Two dramatic tracks of world history are unfolding, one secular, the other spiritual, although this contrast must not be overdrawn or overstated. There is the drama of the United Nations with its massive global power blocs, and the drama of the Middle East, where God has regathered dispersed Israel—in unbelief, as the Bible forewarns—and where all those long-forgotten once-great powers of the past are being resurrected from the dust to world prominence—Iran, Saudi Arabia, Iraq, Syria, Lebanon, with Russia poised virtually at their borders.

The Bible speaks of a recovery of faith by a remnant of Jewry, perhaps by a considerable remnant, and of Messiah's return in such a time.

God often uses wicked powers to punish other powers that have had more light before he in turn destroys them; that holds awesome possibilities for America, Soviet Russia and mainland China also. It is still true that righteousness is the best guarantee to national survival; military might can hold off predator powers but it does not guarantee the future.

Q. Since you have completed your six-volume masterwork on *God, Revelation and Authority*, what will you write next?

A. There's a notable shift in the contemporary mindset—although evangelical campuses seem less aware of it than others—an awakening interest in a reasoned view of life. A number of educators and friends are pressing me to do a Christian worldlife view volume vis-à-vis the present secular alternatives. That's a demanding task, but some things may be said for it.

Q. What do you now consider some of the decisive theological turns?

A. The collapse of antiintellectualistic neoorthodoxy, which rules out objectifying theological statements about God, and of positivism, which limited true and meaningful statements to empirical testability; this helps to shape a new day for evangelical theism. Darwinian evolution is undergoing more trenchant criticism than at any time since the beginning of the century. The doctrine of divine providence needs to illumine anew such catastrophic developments as Auschwitz and the perverse trust in Marxist analysis of history.

Q. What are the biggest disappointments of your lifetime?

A. Evangelical failure to establish a truly great interdenominational university; fragmentation of the evangelical movement just when we might have decisively impacted upon contemporary American life; deployment of *Christianity Today* from its role of serious theological leadership and cultural confrontation.

Q. What strengths has evangelical Christianity?

A. Its ready affirmation of the supernatural amid rampant modern naturalism; its unapologetic emphasis on revealed truths in an age of intellectual skepticism; its awareness of divine moral commands in a time of ethical relativity; its lifechanging dynamic in a generation whose human existence has turned sour and often bitter; its evangelistic passion in a world that acts as if it had no soul.

Q. What are the weaknesses?

A. Reluctance to consider justice and higher education as much a priority as evangelism; rivalry, opportunism and personality-cultism; exaggeration of success to attract funding; undue deference by some leaders to monied supporters; failure to speak powerfully to national conscience and to the cultural millieu; nonpreservation of institutions and neglect of Christian worldlife concerns.

Q. Do you think evangelicals could still recover a significant initiative in the American context, and what would be involved?

A. It will not be achieved through a least-common-denominator evangelicalism that leaves people increasingly in doubt as to what an authentic evangelical is. Yet if evangelical leaders could meet and draw up an agenda of priorities and concentrate on their commonalities rather than their differences they could forge an influential consensus within our secular society.

There will also be clashpoints. But despite differences over baptism, ecclesiology and eschatological secondaries, evangelicals have been able to mount a spectacular evangelistic and missionary leadership that gave them eminence in these areas; so too they ought to be able to mount an exemplary initiative in the public arena.

Q. What accounts for the present confusion and conflict in evangelical ranks?

A. Theologically, of course, the tumult is due to a loosely-knit company of teachers who break with propositional revelation or with plenary inspiration of the Bible or who make critical concessions concerning scriptural authority and hermeneutics.

If the first half of this century teaches us anything it is that, unless arrested, the sad end of that process is irreconcilable confusion. These mediating scholars emphasize that evangelicals "use" the Bible in a variety of ways; their debatable assumption is that one can remain an evangelical, regardless of a perverse use of Scripture.

Q. What about cross currents in the public arena?

A. We can discern, I think a pattern: (1) the timidity of the evangelical establishment; (2) the initiative of a courageous spokesman who mounts a somewhat extreme or unguarded position; (3) the consequent division of evangelicals by way of reaction.

We might mention as examples several important areas where establishment evangelicals should have taken a vigorous initiative but failed to do so; protest against the relativization of moral absolutes in national life; use of television both as an educational and evangelistic medium; emphasis on the importance of creation-doctrine in the public schools; the horrendous proliferation of abortion; the fallaway from biblical authority in erstwhile evangelical circles.

In each of these areas individuals ventured to speak and act where the evangelical movement so-called did not: Jerry Falwell and the Moral Majority; Pat Robertson and others identified as the electronic church; Henry Morris and Creation Research Society; the Pro-Life Movement with its hostility to abortion under any circumstances; and the Lindsell-Schaeffer denunciation of noninerrantists. Somebody needed to speak and act, and in the absense of concerted evangelical action individual spokesmen ventured into the gap.

Although some of these individuals spoke out with courage and initiative, their somewhat extreme or unguarded positions became controversial among evangelicals themselves. The Creation Research Society, for example, linked creation with recency of the earth and flood geology. Others did battle with "false evangelicals" rather than inconsistent evangelicals. Evangelical consensus must preserve what is valid in such protests but escape the extremes of individuals.

Q. What do you consider the role of the evangelical colleges and seminaries?

A. In an age when university learning has lost a cohesive center—in terms of an unchanging God and fixed moral values—the evangelical campuses have the grand opportunity of exhibiting the comprehensive unity of truth and indispensable importance of mind, conscience, godliness and love.

If evangelicals lose the battle for the mind of contemporary man it will be in their own colleges. Proclaiming the imperative of personal commitment is the task of the churches and evangelists. In many cases, however, they press for decision on too narrow an intellectual strip. Conversions among secularly steeped students are comparatively few, and follow-up statistics not good, except where students are intellectually serious. But the evangelists can hardly be expected to compensate for the lack of doctrinal and expository preaching in the churches.

When the colleges emphasize not the intellectual fruits of their effort, but their evangelistic vitality or contribution, in order to encourage constituency support, they merely hide their failure to fulfill their distinctive mission. On some campuses—may their tribe increase—administration and some faculty do indeed see this distinction. Such a school is commendably concerned—and without any implication of ecclesial triumphalism—not simply to expose the weaknesses of nonbiblical alternatives, but to understand also why they address the contemporary mindset as they do, and to detail the specific superiority of evangelical theism. If we are to make a turning-impact, young evangelicals must become lovers of books and of truth; we need more tough-minded scholars to do battle with the intellectual philistines of our day as Augustine and Luther and Calvin did in theirs.

Q. What of the seminaries?

A. They must call to account—in view of God's own revelation—what the churches preach and teach about God who makes Himself and His purposes known in Scripture. Yet today many seminaries hold a broken view of the Bible and the local churches stand in judgment upon them. This situation is not really remedied by new alignments that shape struggling new seminaries because the fragmentation is merely extended and denunciation tends to overarch the church's message. A shattering divine impact, one that renews His people in the awe of God and in reverance for His authority and word, can bring the seminaries and churches again to a role of powerful leadership.

As things are, most seminaries and churches pose little threat to a blatantly secular society; they are tolerated by the secular mindset, much as a grandmother who no longer knows what day of the week it is, or what to do next.

The seminaries are too often infused by worldly ambitions—size, endowment, electronic gadgetry, public relations. They too seldom recognize that just one Solzhenitsyn who speaks the truth boldly and is ready to suffer the consequences may put them permanently on the map in terms of their real mission. The danger is that evangelical ecclesialism may fossilize into a harmless dinosaur rather than survive as a culture-confronting giant.

Q. Doesn't that sound judgmental?

A. I do not intend it thus, and if it seems so, I am sorry. My heart aches at times that the seminaries really do not know the time of the day, that it is virtually midnight for America and perhaps for the world. So often young people come with hearts aflame to learn how most effectively to bear witness to the world in our time and in a few short years they are defused of this passion. The percentage who do not finish their course, or who become vocational dropouts, seems of little concern to their mentors.

Q. Bill Bright of Campus Crusade has said that you were the only professor in all his seminary studies who ever mentioned in class your dealing personally with anyone about the need of faith in Christ?

A. I don't think that every seminary classroom should be turned into a course in evangelism but there's something wrong if divinity professors consider their courses so irrelevant to fulfillment of the Great Commission, or their vocation so unrelated to leading people to knowledge of Christ, that nowhere in the span of a year's teaching do students get any glimpse of personal concern for the lost.

Q. Billy Graham and you have each filled an important role in the fortunes of American evangelism. Where have you differed?

A. Dr. Graham's place in church history is assured; nobody has done more since midcentury to stimulate the evangelistic energies of Christian churches around the world. He has left to others the cause of human rights, including religious liberty. He could have been more decisive in avoiding the forfeiture of a great transdenominational evangelical university and in shaping outcomes at *Christianity Today*. Like many others, Graham is too busy to be present when some critical decisions are won or lost. The role of the Graham Center is still rather ambiguous.

The risks of Graham's Soviet evangelistic aspirations are highly explosive. On the other hand, Soviet leaders little sense the possible explosive consequences of a massive underground spiritual awakening amid a younger generation that is weary of having atheism stuffed down its throat while the case for Christianity cannot be presented on its own merits. But if Graham is allowed a few showcase appearances in Russia, while those Russians who live there are deprived of religious liberty and imprisoned when they seek to do what Graham is allowed for a short span to do, that will be no victory either for justice or for grace.

But here one can only do what he does in good conscience; Graham's objectives are not—as some critics imply—wholly self-serving, since the global preaching of the Gospel is a mandate, and nobody has in our time assumed its risks more than Graham. (*Religious Broadcasting*, December 1982.)

In much of Christendom, today is marked as Good Friday, the day on which Jesus was crucified, and historically for Christians their faith's darkest moment. But on the third day following Jesus' death, the word was going around that "He is risen!" This truth had a stunning effect on those who followed Jesus, impacting history in a way that no other event has ever done.

It is at the Easter season, the most spiritually-significant time of the year for Christians, that some of their deepest reflections on life and its meaning are engaged in, from theologians to the garden variety of believer.

Dr. Carl F.H. Henry is one of the 20th century's influential theologians. Author of 27 books and editor of a dozen others, he served (1947-1956) on the founding faculty of one of the world's largest divinity schools, Fuller Theological Seminary in California, and was founding editor (1956-1968) of the nation's largest evangelical thought magazine, *Christianity Today*.

Chairman of the 1966 World Congress on Evangelism in Berlin, he has been called "the thinking man's Billy Graham." He is author of the six-volume work, *God, Revelation and Authority*, available also in Mandarin and in Korean. As lecturer-at-large for World Vision International, he has addressed leaders and students on all the continents. He was interviewed by *Washington Times* Religious News Editor William F. Willoughby.

Easter: Decisive for the Christian Faith

Q. How do you read the times in which we live?
Dr. Henry. Many people are grasping for hope; some are half-stifled by fear of hopelessness. There's a deep hole in the heart of humanity. It reflects the mediocrity of life, especially among those who have forsaken the inherited truths and values and now find human survival bewildering. Those who have every material reason to be happy seldom are; the more they possess, the more they want, or think they need. Some turn for excitement to an insane mischief—drugs or whatever.

The poor and the well-to-do alike long for a faith that gives hope. Jacques Ellul remarks how desperately we need "a landmark, a North Star . . . to pull us out of the gray-on-grayness of everyday life." What will fill this existential vacuum?
Q. Have you a clue?
A. Nazis exploited this longing and Communists still do even if life in their own societies get duller by the year. Deluded masses lend themselves to the so-called "people's cause" and unwittingly invite a police state and a *gulag*. Much world politics unfortunately breeds a mistrust that readies persons for the Grand Lie. Politicians make vain promises and arouse false hopes only to disillusion the masses. The next totalitarian "benefactor" will be armed with data processing omniscience and with nuclear missiles.
Q. Then is hope an illusion and politics a deception?
A. I didn't say that. God still works providentially in history. Political dynamisms still remain the instrumentality through which God intends rulers to promote justice. And where democratic processes exist they offer live opportunities to share constructively in political outcomes.

But government cannot in any event be our salvation. The

deepest loneliness in human life is due to man's loss of God. The only real hope for security lies in a commitment to God's future. A radically-secular society stops short of that commitment because it demands too much in the way of moral and spiritual decision.

Q. Does it really make a difference that most Americans believe there is a God?

A. For many Americans, yes. Close the churches and synagogues and banish the Bible, prohibit public evangelism, staff the universities only with atheists (as totalitarian rulers would prefer) and the temper of our society would change swiftly.

Religious liberty has been a boon for the American spirit. Yet there is a secular swath of our society whose mindset against supernatural commitments is hardening into an atheistic *willset*.

This stance has been nurtured by the dominance of liberal arts learning for half a generation by radically secular humanism. The naturalistic outlook leads to a shift and inversion of values. Contemporary fiction, television and the cinema become potent instrumentalities for a seductive revision of the established standards. Values that the Judeo-Christian heritage treasures (monogamous marriage, fidelity, chastity) are viewed as enslaving obstacles to self-fulfillment. This warped view of life empties into a disenchanting glory.

Q. Does the Bible address the crucial contemporary concerns?

A. It addresses many modern concerns in precept and others in principle, and it stipulates the "good life" that God commends. The Bible is still the most incisive critic of our age. It confronts our broken love of God, our dull sense of justice, our shameful moral nakedness, our waning sense of ethical duty, our badly-numbed consciences, our clutching anxieties, the ghastly horrors and brutal violence of this era.

The biblical prophets are far from outmoded; they are far ahead of us. They provide landmarks that we need more than ever in the dense forests of subjectivism to which modern speculation abandons us. If God is the source and sum of all justice, if the line between good and evil cannot be shaded, if we remain eternally responsible for the decisions we make in this life, as the Bible attests, then its sobering message deserves the highest national priority.

Easter: Decisive for the Christian Faith 127

It recognizes the legitimate role of civil government in deterring predator powers, yet warns us against ultimate trust in weaponry. It emphasizes the dignity and worth of every human life, yet emphasizes that physical survival is not the highest of all values. And it gives us reason and motivation for getting involved in public affairs.

Q. Now that the globe is an international village, don't universal claims for any one religion seem outdated?

A. I know very well the claim that all religions are false or that none has truth-status. Usually such claims are made by those who promote a masked absolute of their own. We ought indeed to pursue dialogue between adherents of all religions.

Christianity, at any rate, has no divine mandate to destroy other world religions by the sword. You know, of course, that Feuerbach and Marx both thought that by our time Christianity would lie buried with the Homeric myths, and that some exuberant naturalists have claimed that scientific knowledge explains God away.

Christianity has meanwhile become the first religion to gain a world presence, even in some Asian and African countries it has become the fastest growing force. Where communism tries to extirpate it or to drive it underground, it becomes purified and deepens its commitments. In Latin America those who profess it anew are largely the working class.

Unlike Buddhism, Christianity does not put a premium on self-extinction, nor does it, like Hinduism, treat human life as a mere transmigratory phenomenon, nor is it like much of Islam, in flight from the realities of this world, nor does it protect itself by denying others the right to change their religion. The great distinctive of Christianity is the person and work of Jesus Christ who lifts the whole conception of divine revelation to a new order.

Q. Yet we and our children must live in a world of conflicting beliefs, must we not?

A. Many rival beliefs, indeed—philosophical, scientific, religious; the world is surfeited by them. Man cannot live without beliefs. The Free World is now too divided intellectually, too weak morally, too dimsighted spiritually, to project an overarching global outlook.

Some observers see American society now engaged in a tug-of-war between three competing worldviews: materialism, mysticism and biblical theism. Scientists and philosophers continue to have more beliefs than they care to admit.

Shadow beliefs are no less important in mobilizing people for good or ill than are expressly acknowledged beliefs. (Is honesty in scientific research, for example, merely a personal option?) Never has the question been more important whether our beliefs are simply scientific tentatives, speculative conjecture, private psychic certitudes, or universally-valid truth.

The Christian believes—and for good reason—that God has spoken and that He has made known His will and purpose, and that in view of divine revelation certain truths are final and moral principles unchanging. One's belief-spectrum colors all else: one's view of society, politics, culture, technology and the arts.

Q. How, for example, might worldview differences bear on some specific modern concerns?

A. The mother who aborts a fetus with a handicap and the mother who showers love on a handicapped child have different worldlife views. The mother who abandons an unwanted child has a worldview different from the mother who believes no child should be unwanted.

The lover who doesn't tell his fiance that he carries a recessive gene for Tay-Sachs disease or that he has herpes has a worldlife view different from the lover who thinks his intended mate ought to know all the risks to which he will expose her.

The professor who trades grades for sex has a worldlife view different from the professor who thinks all students should be judged by academic standards.

It makes a difference if we think ourselves to be merely self-seeking animals or fellow participants in a society answerable to divine justice, if we think nature is ours to manipulate or if we are responsible caretakers of the cosmos.

A worldview based on naturalistic evolution can provide no rational foundation for universal or permanent human rights; in fact, naturalism has no logical basis for validating any norms whatever.

Q. Isn't freedom becoming a mask for self-interest?

A. All the great value-words, like liberty, truth, justice and the good, are loaded today with conflicting and even con-

Easter: Decisive for the Christian Faith   129

tradictory meanings. But counterfeits always presuppose an authentic original. There's all the more need today to ring the bells for authentic freedom, because so much of human existence bears the marks of enslavement on the one hand, and so many on the other hand turn freedom into a normless liberation that entails a worsened slavery and even personal nihilism.

Tolerance becomes a cliche that caters to our weaknesses, violence is welcomed as the way to promote values. Religious liberty becomes a disguise for advancing atheism and a device for escaping the question of truth in religious claims. There is a very real danger that modern civilization will disintegrate and that we will be part of its debris.

Q. Easter—how much is myth and how much is fact?

A. The bunny, colored eggs and jelly beans are so much confetti. Easter is Jesus Christ or it is nothing. Jesus claimed to be the singular Son of God. If he was self-deceived, we can hardly credit his lesser claims about God's purposes and commands. The Gospels deny that he was a mere man, even the superlatively good man.

The New Testament alternatives reduce to the God-man or to a blasphemer and deceiver. These alternatives divided those who crucified him and those who worshipped him.

Easter Sunday—marking the bodily resurrection of the crucified Jesus—is the turning event that finally is decisive for the Christian faith. The Roman military force officially sealed the tomb. The guards, aided by the Sanhedrin round-the-clock lest the tomb be violated, conceded that the body had disappeared.

On the assumption that the disciples had stolen Jesus' body and hidden the corpse, the brilliant young theologian, Saul of Tarsus, was accredited by the high priest and other religious leaders to pursue the early Christians. When the risen Jesus, who had previously appeared time and again to his disciples, also appeared to Saul of Tarsus, the great Jewish religionist became an apostle of Jesus Christ to the whole Gentile world as well as to Jewry.

The heart of the Christian faith, Paul writes, is that "Christ died for our sins according to the Scriptures, was buried and raised again the third day, according to the Scriptures, and was seen . . ." (I Cor. 15:3-4). (*The Washington Times*, April 1, 1983.)

Dr. Carl F.H. Henry is a world renowned scholar and leading evangelical theologian. The founding editor of *Christianity Today*, he has authored 27 books, and edited a dozen others. He graduated from Wheaton in 1939, and returned to our campus last week for the Thomas F. Staley Distinguished Scholar Lectureship.

In the following interview, by Pau Woo, Henry shares some of his views on Wheaton, evangelicalism, and higher learning.

Wheaton and the Evangelicals

Q. Dr. Henry, you had a Wheaton education over forty years ago. Can you give us an idea of what it was like back then?
Dr. Henry. When I came to Wheaton, there was in the air the possibility of moving towards a Christian university. Dr. J. Oliver Buswell was himself an intellectual and he was thinking to lift Scholastic Honor Society so that it would attain Phi Beta Kappa status. You need to have a certain number of profs who are Phi Betas to be eligible, and I think he was within three professors at the time that he was asked to resign from the presidency because of the controversy with the Presbyterian church.

But there was a deep scholarly commitment and also a deep missionary commitment on this campus. In those days, the evangelical movement was conspicuously a minority movement, and modernism and humanism were struggling with each other for the fortunes of Christianity.

We had just put in a master's program in theology and it was a very exciting time to be here. It was also the aftermath of the depression, and it was too expensive for us not to take our learning opportunity seriously.
Q. Was and is Wheaton the vanguard of evangelical higher learning?
A. Well, Calvin College was in the earlier years much more markedly a Christian Reformed center. I think Calvin has exercised a growing, shaping influence. Wheaton has grown, and it has continued to make an immense contribution to the evangelical movement throughout the world, but much more in the area of evangelism and missions than in the area of intellectual leadership or book publications.

Also, I think Wheaton has made an excellent contribution to the medical profession, and in the recent past, it has made an accelerated contribution in the area of political science and law.

Q. You made a statement at chapel on Monday—"that the younger generation should give rise to leadership in learning"—is this a call for Wheaton students to take up scholastic careers?

A. Yes, I think so, because if Wheaton takes seriously being the largest Christian liberal arts college with commitments beyond the undergraduate level, then in the world of modern learning, the wrestling of ideas and the battle for the minds of men is an inescapable duty.

This is a time of cultural confusion. If the Christian point of view is going to be presented relevantly, by whom will it be presented, if not by alumni of schools specializing in Christian thought?

I've always thought it strange that the Jews in Israel could, in such a remarkably short time, shape a great Hebrew university in Jerusalem. The Roman Catholics also have their massive Catholic universities, but the evangelicals in America—55 million of them—have not been able to get together to plan a great metropolitan school with colleges in the various disciplines of learning.

I don't think Wheaton will ever change that now. I don't think the trustees are interested in a Christian university and I'm not saying that they should be, but Wheaton will be able to make contributions in special areas where there are existing needs.

Q. To this end, which developments do you see are essential for Wheaton College? Perhaps, for example, new departments? A law school?

A. Well, I think these decisions will have to be made by the administration and the faculty and the financial resources that the school has. More important than that is the question of overall comprehensive vision, and I think the school will either move gradually in an exploratory way, or it will require a canopy vision on a long-range basis. With the mounting costs of education today, this doesn't seem like a very propitious time for launching of that sort of canopy.

Q. How do you feel evangelicalism has kept up with the trends of our recent history?

A. I think the evangelical movement has shown a remarkable dynamic and resilience in our time, and there is no question of the profound indebtedness to Billy Graham for the evangelistic impact that was registered on the denominations. I think the growth in college and seminary enrollments, and the dedication in the evangelistic and missionary tasks worldwide, are all high assets of the movement.

I think the movement looks stronger than it is because of the weakness of ecumenical Protestantism and because of the conflicts that have been evident within Roman Catholicism. I also think the evangelical establishment—the formative forces that are positioned financially and structurally to take the leadership—has been too timid in charting directions in controversial frontiers.

Q. What is your reaction, then, to the response of the religious right?

A. I'm glad that evangelicals are politically involved. I'm glad that evangelicals have come out of the subculture into the culture, even though sometimes greatly troubled. But the way in which some of them do it sometimes troubles me. I find it difficult for evangelicals who organize political hit squads to be associated at the same time with the proclamation of the Gospel of love.

It seems to me we need a whole lot more finesse and skill, and that the evangelicals unfortunately are often battling each other in the public arena rather than seeking out the areas of agreement and consensus. Certainly there is a large span of commonalities that evangelicals share over against the secular political order.

Q. In the editorial of the February issue of *Christianity Today*, Kenneth Kantzer presented a list of problems within the evangelical movement. Three related points were the combative lifestyle, reactionary tendencies, and a house divided. If his diagnosis is right, does this mean that evangelicals should work more closely with those who do not share similar theological positions?

A. Evangelicals should work for certain ends with anybody who is identified with those goals, irrespective of what their theological or non-theological commitments are. When you work in the public sector, you work with fellow citizens for the life of the nation. The trouble with many evangelicals is that they seek to put all their eggs in one basket.

At the same time, when we speak in a corporate evangelical effort, we ought to make sure that what we advance is authentically evangelical. In the political arena, there is room for differences of opinion. There is no reason to question the evangelical authenticity of someone who disagrees with another on some issue.

Q. But isn't there a "Quest for Purity" in the evangelical movement? William Hutchinson of Harvard University, who was here recently for the Evangelicalism History Conference, brought up the point that while there was a call at Harvard Divinity School for an evangelical chair, there were no similar calls for liberal chairs at Gordon-Conwell or Dallas.

A. Well, I think there is a real need in the evangelical movement to search its self-consciousness on the issues of truth and purity. If the evangelicals lose their schools, it will probably be from within. If the evangelical churches lose their cultural impact, it will be because they lose their distinctiveness and become what some of the non-evangelical churches became—social service clubs or spiritual Rotary clubs. Then people become evangelicals for the wrong reasons.

Q. You have often been described as "the thinking man's Billy Graham." How do you react to that?

A. Well, I should think Billy Graham would not be flattered. I suppose what it intends to say is that I have a commitment to evangelism as Billy Graham does, but that I think that the implication of evangelism must be couched so that we engage the whole world of modern learning at the crucual cognitive frontiers.

Q. As a leading evangelical theologian, what do you think is the relevance of theology to the so-called "secular" disciplines?

A. It is either the king or queen of the sciences. The modern tendency is to discard theology from any reign whatsoever. We want to take it out to the nearest dockside and discard it as diversionary truth. But I think theology is radioactive, and if you attempt to discard it, it will stay around to raise the question of the worth and meaning of human survival.

Everyone has a theology. It may be a very shoddy one, and if it is shoddy, it will rise to haunt one in a crisis of life. It's my conviction that only a theology which has the living God at its center and that is rooted in Christ, the crucified and risen Redeemer, has the intellectual struts to engage the modern secular views effectively. (*Wheat on Record*, May 6, 1983.)

Cornerstone, magazine of the Jesus people, interviews Dr. Carl F.H. Henry.

Founding editor of *Christianity Today* magazine and author of over twenty-eight books, including the six-volume landmark, *God, Revelation, and Authority*, theologian Dr. Henry is viewed by many as evangelical Christianity's most articulate and thoughtful spokesman. Currently Dr. Henry is lecturer at large for World Vision and distinguished visiting professor of Christian Studies at Hillsdale College (Michigan). In this *Cornerstone* interview he reveals an aspect of our relationship to God rarely discussed and often misunderstood.

Shall We Fear God?

Q. Is fear of God really a proper response—ideally and normatively—to the true God?
Dr. Henry. Yes and no. The term covers a semantic span from reverence to terror. If we are speaking of reverential awe of God's glory and majesty, then every finite creature should fear him. But if we mean moral fear in view of God's righteousness, then it's noteworthy that the Bible makes no reference to man's fear before the fall of Adam. After the fall, Adam—a sinner with a bad conscience—says: "I heard thy voice in the garden and I was afraid" (Gen. 3:10). For good reason Adam feared God in the aftermath of a ruptured fellowship consequent upon his sin.
Q. Then sinful human beings should now fear God both because of his majesty and because of his righteousness?
A. Surely because of his majesty: the great emphasis of the biblical wisdom literature is that "the fear of the Lord is the beginning of wisdom" (Ps. 111:10). Some of the biblical proverbs suggest that fear of the Lord is prerequisite to a proper knowledge of him (Prov. 2:5, 9:10). New Testament Christians walked in the fear of the Lord (Acts 9:31).
Q. Do you imply, however, that sinners should not live in fear of God?
A. Impossible. Jesus said that impenitent sinners should fear God who has power to cast the wicked into hell (Luke 12:1-5). Our secular Western society neither loves God nor does it much fear him, but it cannot wholly escape a fearsome sense of coming judgement. Moral rebels and impenitent sinners—including atheists—live in unpublished fear of God. The apostle Paul writes that "they know God's decree, that those who do such things deserve to die" (Rom. 8:15) since they remain under condemnation of God's law. In the eschatological future—the end-time, the book of Revelation says, the fearful are the unbelieving. But in the life of the penitent believer fear has a somewhat more complex role—different in Old Testa-

ment and New Testament, and differing even in our day in the life and experience of the people of God.

Q. Can you unpack that complexity a bit for us?

A. Well, the New Testament, because of the internalization of the redemptive work of Christ and of God's covenant ("I shall write my law upon their hearts") views believers as adopted children of God. Paul writes Timothy that "God did not give us a spirit of fear (timidity) but a spirit of power and love and self-control" (II Tim. 1:7); a better reference, on second thought, is Hebrews 4:16, which exhorts us to come boldly to God's throne of grace. In the Old Testament, prior to messianic fulfillment of the sacrificial system, the plan of worship emphasized divine distance from sinful mankind. We shouldn't exaggerate the contrast, however, to imply that fear of God in biblical Judaism was displaced by love of God in biblical Christianity.

Fear of God in the Old Testament did not cancel intimate fellowship with God (as anyone who treasures the Psalms knows full well: "I will fear no evil, for thou art with me" (Ps. 23:4). Nor does New Testament experience actually lift the believer to a wholly fearless existence in this life (for sanctification is progressive and in any event is not yet glorification). Although Jesus Christ fully conquered fear both in principle and practice, for us the total abolition of fear waits for the life to come.

Q. Does that then put Christians on the same ground with unbelievers?

A. Not really. The Christian in whose life God is redemptively at work knows that since we are God's, and Christ has borne our sin and guilt, there is no need to fear God our Father, yet he works out his salvation "with fear and trembling" (Phil. 2:12) aware that "perfect love casts our fear" (I John 4:18). The work of redemption evokes a hatred of evil (Prov. 8:13). The unbeliever, at his faithless best, knows that man's whole duty is to "fear God and keep his commandments" (Ec. 12:13), yet he trusts no mediator although his faulty works cannot satisfy what a righteous God requires; he can only hope, vainly, that God is tolerant of sin.

Q. Is fear of God really any longer a surface phenomenon in secular society today?

A. For a half century secular moderns have increasingly seen themselves as a new kind of humanity, whose fulfillment lay not in fear of God and spiritual obedience but in an eclipse and avoidance of the supernatural. Franklin D. Roosevelt, in his third inaugural address, fancied a world entirely free from fear: fear itself, he said, is what we need most to fear. But no act of political magic or verbal voodoo can banish human fear. Our generation consumes huge quantities of sedatives, barbituates, and other tranquilizers in moot testimony to its haunting anxieties. The recreant who concedes he's "scared as hell" isn't impoverished by language nearly as much as he is self-deprived of the joys of heaven. Before our age of so-called miracle medicines a noted Bible commentator translated the Isaian reference to "the Prince of Peace" to read "the Tranquilizer." Jesus offered his disciples peace such as he knew even on the way to crucifixion—and it wasn't a prescription for Valium. Ours is a self-gratifying generation spooked by secret guilt and fears. Ask the psychiatrists: multitudes of moderns think the way to "stop running scared" is to see a shrink. They distrust their own shadows because they no longer are sure who they are. Some fear the future like a cancer.

Q. How are we to confront a society prone to forsake God and given to self-sufficiency?

A. Remember the pit from which we were digged and extend a helping hand. Many Christians now live among neighbors who, swept by tides of immorality, fear herpes more than they fear Hades and some even think God is a lofty synonym for gobbledygook. We must love them and live as show windows on the high privilege and reward of knowing the Lord of life. The world does not much see Christians on their knees before God any more; in fact, Christians all too seldom see each other bent low in the presence of the Holy One. The Bible must become priority reading for us and for this generation; it confronts the wrong fears and inculcates fear of God, fear of unregeneracy, fear of stealing, of adultery, and much else. But it goes far beyond all that. In his hymn, "There is a Land of Pure Delight," Isaac Watts put it aptly: "When I can read my title clear, To mansions in the skies, I bid farewell to every fear, And wipe my weeping eyes."

Q. Life on our planet seems to have an unsure future—why so?
A. Because human security and serenity are found in God alone and multitudes are trying to get along without him. Solzhenitsyn says that "men have forgotten God" and that the 20th century civilizational crisis is a consequence of this. We live amid the first effort in the long history of the West to erect human culture on godless foundations.
Q. Has contemporary man no fear of God?
A. The totalitarian atheists are God-defiers (they persecute and disadvantage believers in supernatural theism). The humanist atheists are God-deniers (they eagerly lampoon the supernatural as legend). The practical atheists are God-detractors (they treat God as if he were dead). The rest of us tend to give the living God a bad press (our words speak louder than our lives). The resurgent evangelical movement has too much tamed its fear of God; it sometimes performs triumphally as if it had the Lion of the tribe of Judah by the tail, and as if Christ were serving us rather than our serving him.
Q. Are you pessimistic or optimistic about the future?
A. I'm an eternal optimist because eternity is in God's hands. But the immediate future is now in the making and it may be bleak or bright. There is no Marxian inevitability about history, that's for sure. The biblical truths and values still remain the great moving forces of history; either they will capture us or we shall be judged by them.

Many social critics write of the decline and stagnation and decay and even imminent death of Western civilization, of a culture will not mean the end of God; it could be the preface the root of all this. One thing is sure—the doom of modern culture will not mean the end of God; it would be the preface to or underside of spiritual awakening. But the tragedy is that the culture itself, purified and renewed, could survive as one of the great eras in the moral and spiritual history of mankind. (*Cornerstone,* May 1, 1984.)

Dr. Carl F.H. Henry, a noted theologian and author, was founding editor of *Christianity Today* magazine, is a visiting professor of Christian studies at Hillsdale College in Michigan, and is a lecturer-at-large for World Vision, a global humanitarian agency. He has completed a multivolume work, *God, Revelation, and Authority*, that is available in Mandarin, Korean and English. His 28th book, *The Christian Mindset in a Secular Society*, has just been published by Multnomah Press. Dr. Henry, now of Arlington, Virginia, was interviewed by Joe Gillette for *The Washington Times*.

The Resurrection Is What Life Is All About
Easter and Its Meaning

Q. Is Easter losing its hold on the American consciousness?
Dr. Henry. Among spiritual vagabonds probably, and surely among an atheistic hard-core, but not for multitudes of Americans who seriously reflect on questions of death and an afterlife.
Q. You believe, then, that the importance of Easter stands or falls with the resurrection of Jesus of Nazareth?
A. Precisely: The resurrection of the crucified Jesus is what is at stake. The apostle Paul put the matter squarely: If Christ is not risen, then faith in him is futile.
Q. Is a bodily resurrection in ordinary history any longer credible?
A. Nothing in science or in philosophy precludes it, and the evidence in the case of Jesus is considered persuasive even by many brilliant legal minds. "Ordinary history" isn't all that ordinary; it is a flow of events in which God works out moral and spiritual purposes. And Jesus of Nazareth was not just "anybody"; the death and resurrection of the Messiah was foretold in the Old Testament, and was reaffirmed by Jesus during his public ministry.
Q. How does this belief in the resurrection and in what Easter portends have bearing on the modern day?
A. Many people are grasping for hope; some are half-stifled by fear of hopelessness. There's a deep hole in the heart of humanity. It reflects the mediocrity of life, especially among those who have forsaken the inherited truths and values and now find human survival bewildering. Those who have every material reason to be happy seldom are; the more they want, the more they think they need. The poor and the well-to-do alike long for a faith that gives hope.

Q. What does Jesus' resurrection imply for human immortality?
A. Everything. First, that the whole self—not just some psychic or mental remnant—is somehow involved in an afterlife. Second, that much more is involved than life in a new kind of body suited to existence in the world to come, because moral and spiritual issues are crucial.
Q. What do you mean by that?
A. The heart of Christian doctrine is that "Christ died for our sins" and that humans face a dual destiny in eternity conditioned on their individual relationships to the Redeemer.
Q. For many centuries secular philosophers preferred the theory that the soul or mind of man survives death and that immortality has nothing to do with bodily resurrection, did they not?
A. The classic ancient Greek view was that man's mind is inherently divine and therefore indestructible. Christians knew better; man, although in God's image, is a finite creature in every iota of his being. The Greek view lost philosophical credibility early in this century. Freud emphasized the deep, dark recesses of the human subconscious. After contemporary man, whom secular philosophers considered essentially good, ventured World War I and World War II and even Auschwitz, nobody could any longer believe in the intrinsic divinity (and hence indestructability) of the human psyche. Today the alternatives for secular thought and for Christian thought are either the crematory or cemetery, or resurrection life as man's final destination.
Q. What is the meaning of Good Friday?
A. Luther called it "black Friday"—when the foul hands of wicked humans nailed the sinless Christ to a tree and executed him. But the resurrection reversal of the destructive intentions of that crime not only vindicated Jesus' claims to messianity, but in God's providence also exhibited the sinless Jesus as the holy substitute or savior who died for penitent sinners.
Q. You speak like a proponent, like a disciple.
A. I am.
Q. Were you born a Christian?
A. Far from it. My parents were nominal Christians but in our home we had no prayer, no grace at the table, no Bible. The

The Resurrection Is What Life Is All About   145

first Bible I ever read I pilfered from the pew racks of a church where we children attended Sunday school.

Q. Weren't you a journalist before you became a believer?

A. Yes. In high school I was a sports reporter, and five years later became editor of a weekly paper on Long Island, and also suburban stringer in Suffolk County, New York, for the *New York Herald Tribune, Daily News* and *Standard News Association* and later for *The New York Times*.

Q. What interested you in Jesus Christ?

A. Interested me? I was covertly running away from him—like many of my contemporaries. I went through the ritual—the outward forms, like baptism, confirmation, even communion, but it was like a charade, although I thought I was sincere. But one day a young university alumnus asked if I knew what Christ can do with a life wholly given to him, and made an appointment to chat with me about it.

Q. What did you do?

A. I broke the appointment three times, because its religious overtones made me uncomfortable. When I finally kept it, I made a personal commitment. I was and am persuaded that Jesus Christ is alive, and that he communes with his disciples. I would have gone to the ends of the Earth had he spurred me to do so that very day 50 years ago. That's why believers sing, "You ask me how I know He lives? He lives within my heart."

Q. Would it really solve the world's problems if everyone became a Christian?

A. Not if multitudes became merely nominal Christians; part of our problem today is that people put on Christianity like a pair of Totes in rainy weather. But think what it would mean for the world if people lived by the Ten Commandments (no coveting, stealing, murder, adultery), if they practiced the Sermon on the Mount (love for neighbor as for self), if they put God first. Do you know what would happen to police blotters and court dockets and prison statistics?

Q. What do you do with those who would rather suppress the Bible?

A. The Bible actually holds out no hope for world conversion, though God has gone the last mile to redeem and reconcile man. In a fallen world God wills civil government to preserve justice and order and to restrain those who wish by force and violence to bend human history to their perverse ends. Keep your guard up, love them, work with them for common concerns, expose the fallacy of their life-view. Remind them that the empty tomb means they needn't doom themselves to an empty life and to a calamitous judgment to come.

Q. You were for many years chairman or cochairman of the Rose Bowl Easter Sunrise Service. Are such gatherings on the wane?

A. World War II discouraged large gatherings in coastal areas and the cost of gasoline during the energy crisis worked against them, also the fact that in bleak weather people could watch on television. I remember the Soldier Field services in Chicago, where 60,000 persons attended on Easter in weather so cold that someone had to hold an electric light bulb over the hands of the organist to keep them limber. Every generation of believers finds its own ways of witnessing to the realities of faith. (*The Washington Times*, April 20, 1984.)

Carl Henry is the elder statesman of modern evangelical Christianity. A writer and theologian, he has been one of the leaders who has brought this movement from the periphery of life onto main street America.

A strongly committed, Christ-centered, and biblically based thinker, he states the foundation of his philosophy in this way: "The Bible remains the world's most indispensable reading, and a personal walk with God remains man's unsurpassable privilege. All the valid assumptions about the meaning and worth of life and about a just society flow from this."

This interview, conducted by James R. and Elizabeth S. Newby, was included in their volume *Between Peril and Promise* (Nelson, 1984) in which 15 Christian thinkers share their vision for the Church.

Devout Theologian

Q. Dr. Henry, what developments in modern Christianity concern you most?
Dr. Henry. Since Christians have no reason to project millennial expectation upon the world, the woeful political and economic confusion in the world today should not surprise me, but it does concern me. This confusion leads to public events that bear directly and indirectly upon the fortunes of Christians.

The anti-intellectual atmosphere of many evangelical schools and the failure of evangelical scholars to shape a powerful witness to the world of secular learning in a time of civilizational transition are also disconcerting. There are timid evangelical establishment voices in amid mass media opportunities, but their lack of coordination in a unified witness hurts them in the public arena.

Because of this lack of coordination, individuals tend to press into the neglected realms of evangelism, politics, etc., advancing and institutionalizing immoderate programs that tend to divide the evangelical forces. Evangelicals have long cooperated in evangelism and missions, despite doctrinal disagreements over baptism, church government, and glossolalia. If American evangelicals do not likewise shape a coalition around other commonalities, their ingress into the public arena may lead to conflict, confusion, even chaos, and their fortunes may be worse than if they had not made the effort.

The evangelical effort was miscarried, for example, by correlating the issue of biblical authority and inerrancy with diatribe against "false evangelicals," by correlating theistic creation only with recency of the universe and flood-geology, by leaving television evangelism largely to the charismatic electronic church, and by allowing political concerns to be misperceived through calls for the political re-establishment of a Christian nation.

Evangelicals need a comprehensive strategy and a willingness to chart and emphasize commonalities in the midst of their differences.

Q. In your lifetime, what are some of the significant changes through which the church has gone?

A. The list is long. In my time arose:

1. The ecumenical thrust for one great world church, soon dominated by theological pluralism and by ecclesiastical politicization.
2. The emergence of independent, parachurch evangelical forces in rival movements of their own.
3. The failure of neo-Protestant ecumenical efforts to forge a decisive link with Rome.
4. The loss of confidence by local congregations in their ecumenical bureaucracies.
5. The membership decline of major ecumenically oriented denominations.
6. Billy Graham's evangelistic crusades and new focus on global evangelism as the church's unfulfilled mission.
7. The inability of evangelical movements to attract sufficient numbers of fellow evangelicals within the ecumenically oriented churches and their conspicuous link instead with charismatic agencies.
8. The reluctance of some Southern Baptist leaders to use the term *evangelical* as definitive of that constituency.
9. And, consequently, the inability to surmount the disunity of the churches in a pattern that merely merged into larger groupings the erstwhile smaller elements with their separate ailments.

The church, meanwhile, existed in a world environment whose forces were beyond her control and ability to influence effectively—the drift to totalitarianism and away from democratic government, the emergence of the space and media age, the sympathy for revolution at the expense of orderly processes of change, the impact of modern culture on the professing church's ideas and ideals, and the controversy over the role of women in the preaching ministry. All of this has been taking place while the larger concerns of revelation and culture are neglected. There has also been a growing debate over church and state relationships.

Q. Projecting ourselves into the future, what is in store for the church?
A. How shall we define *the church*? Roman Catholicism understands it one way. Protestant ecumenism another. Evangelical Christians mean something very specific: regenerate believers ruled by the risen Lord.

The fortunes of individual believers will vary in the future as they do now, but the believing church as a whole will face both new opportunities and new obstacles in the days ahead. The secular mentality scorns, satirizes, and caricatures the "moral meanies." Secular press and media—skeptical as they are about permanently good news—tend to lump the gospel with the dinosaur age.

For some of this misunderstanding evangelicals have only themselves to blame. They have not enthusiastically channeled dedicated young Christians into the media and other public careers. Jesus warned that the day would come when the world will heap upon His followers the same hatred it displayed toward Him and that some would even think that they "do God a service" by killing the believers. The animosity exhibited toward the people of God in officially atheist lands, and the hostility exhibited toward Christians even in religiously tolerant lands today, cautions us against the platitude that faith in Christ means health, prosperity, and worldly success.

It is only as each Christian generation effectively permeates its environment with biblical moral sensitivities that unregenerate society is restrained from acting on its deep-seated prejudices and is encouraged to judge itself by Christian ideals—even where it is unwilling to embrace those ideals as an explicit intellectual commitment.

Q. What developments in the Christian movement give you hope?
A. What gives hope? The risen Christ's evident power among multitudes of humans whose lives radiate with joy, spiritual vitality, moral earnestness, inner peace, and outgoing love in a melancholy age. All around us we see the frightful cheapness and shocking vulgarity of modern human existence, the hollow reason and numbed conscience of those who refuse to think about God, and the warped consolation drawn from the illusion that we are but pebbles lashed by the chaotic winds of chance-ridden history.

We can take heart that the Christian task force is now deployed worldwide and strategically positioned for its witness. It is familiar with the languages used by a billion pagans and has ready access in the space and media age to virtually all who need to hear the gospel. There's hope in the emergence of erstwhile missionary "receiving" churches as missionary "sending" churches whose Asian and African leaders are providing new evangelistic challenge and stimulus to western Christians. There is also hope in the emphasis at home on the missionary character of the whole church and on the tent-making ministries. These ministries are no less indispensable than professional ministries in the fulfillment of the Great Commission.

I find heartening the emergence of an evangelically dedicated vanguard of university students on secular American campuses despite secular humanism's erosive impact on belief in the supernatural. Likewise, the volunteering by many thousands of Korean college and high school students for a year of evangelistic effort is also encouraging.

In Marxist lands, moreover, the new generation deeply recognizes the dismal failure of communist theory and practice. In the West, there also appear glimmers of a renewed emphasis on the significance of Christ and the Bible for the intellect and a re-affirmation of Christian worldlife view concerns.

No movement in history has at its disposal such human potential and facilities, and such divine resources, as has the Christian movement. American evangelicals have come out of the subculture into the culture, and they are perceived as carriers of spiritual life and ethical earnestness in a time when throngs of humans find life bitter and bewildering.

Q. Is the survival of the church a live question?
A. Destruction of the true church is excluded by Jesus Christ's resurrection, ascension, priestly ministry, and final return. He is the Head of the body—the supernatural source of the church's distinctive life.
Q. How has the church failed in its attempt to win the world and in what ways has it been successful?
A. The phrasing of your question troubles me if it assumes—as some do—that the church is to blame for the world's unbelief.

Devout Theologian 153

The world is guilty before God. Mankind everywhere revolts against God's universal revelation in nature, history, and conscience—a revelation that penetrates the very mind of man. Nor is the church at its best—the church aflame—likely to win the world. Nothing in the Bible encourages the expectation of world conversion or of universal salvation. The New Testament speaks of a pervasive hatred of God.

Yet, the intention of your question is sound: to emphasize the church's duty to fulfill the Great Commission. The notion that the world could be saved from injustice and restored to righteousness by education, legislation, and socialization was the great error of modernist theology. The equally unsound notion that it can attain messianic justice through violence is the mistake of the theology of revolution. The church must proclaim the God of justice and of justification—the self-revealed God who has established civil government for the express promotion of equity and order in a fallen society. This God freely offers forgiveness of sins and new life in Christ to all who repent and trust the Mediator who lived, died, and now lives for us at the Father's right hand.

The church has been successful in the modern era of missions because it has carried the gospel to every nation on earth. But to complete its worldwide task, the church must not rely only on professional missionaries. Instead it must revive both the neglected emphasis that every believer is a missionary, and the tent-making ministries that recognize that God has placed us in our work to witness to our fellow humans.

The spiritual awakening of the local church and the imperative of personal witness by every believer are vital links in the church's world task. The church dares not neglect the media, to be sure, but person-to-person witness remains a biblical mandate.

Q. As you have grown up in the evangelical movement, in what ways are you different now than you were twenty-five years ago?

A. Twenty-five years ago I had less awareness of how readily religious boards buckle under the influence of monied interests, more hope that institutional rivalries could be transcended, more belief in the selflessness of evangelical leaders, and much confidence that evangelical cooperation would forge a Christian worldlife response to secular learning and cooperatively mount a powerful witness in public affairs.

Evangelical leaders and movements were then reaching out creatively, energetically, and cooperatively to speak to a world whose hope was on the wane and to a church weary of ecumenical politicization. Fuller Theological Seminary had brought new challenge to the evangelical movement, Graham crusades escalated evangelism with somewhat of an intellectual tone, and evangelical books addressed doctrinal and ethical dilemmas; there was prospect of a great evangelical transdenominational university.

Q. How about from ten years ago?

A. Ten years ago noteworthy changes had already set in. Fuller Theological Seminary had lost the enthusiasm of its founding faculty, ecumenical resistance to Graham was hardening, *Christianity Today* had begun its movement toward a less theologically oriented magazine of general readership, evangelical colleges were yielding to the anti-intellectual mood of the student world and produced no great text on Christian worldlife theory, and hucksters reaped evangelical book profits while many serious concerns were neglected. Also, while evangelical evangelists crowded the radio channels, they achieved little effective impact through the secular press and left television opportunities largely to experienced-centered spokesmen for the emerging charismatic movement.

At the same time, the evangelical movement was growing. College and seminary enrollments were at a peak. Evangelical evangelism was thriving on secular campuses. Some evangelical publishers were issuing major works of scholarly merit, including new commentaries rather than reprints, and many secular houses welcomed evangelical authors. The growth of World Vision attested that evangelicals were now as fully committed to social concern as to evangelism. The Institute for Advanced Christian Studies enlisted evangelical scholars in serious textbook writing largely neglected by evangelical liberal arts faculties. The transforming power of the evangel was evident in the life of Watergate prisoner Charles Colson and others.

Thereafter, evangelicals became a significant force in the

election of President Carter and then in his defeat, in the election of President Reagan, and in the leadership of the Moral Majority and other movements.

But there is a jockeying for power in evangelical Christianity today that does not bode well for the movement. This calls for spiritual renewal and a new vision of God. In relation to the fortunes of evangelical Christianity, my stance remains fundamentally unchanged. I am fully committed in principle to a biblically oriented, biblically authorized, and biblically controlled faith.

Q. What one word would you use to describe your feelings about the future of Christianity today and why?

A. *Glory*—the destiny toward which the regenerate church moves.

Even now, in the worst of times, the church is prone to resurrection. The Head of the body has already passed through death and resurrection and lives in the eternal order. Even now, he imparts powers and virtues that belong to the coming age, sharing with us a sample of our future inheritance.

To be sure, *Christianity* is a much more ambiguous term than *regenerate church*. But while it shelters much ambiguity on earth, it also leads the devout into the eternal presence of the living God. Buddhism promises to lead one to cessation of individual selfhood, and other religions tell us where they propose to lead us. Jesus Christ promises to lead us into the eternal presence of the Father, and he will make good on his promise.

It may well be that American evangelical leaders who basked in the limelight of news magazine and press coverage of their political influence and moral initiatives in national life will soon be stunned as the movement becomes a wilderness cult with no more public significance in a secular society than the ancient Essenes in the Dead Sea Caves. If so, however, it will not be simply because secular society has forced that fate upon us. It will be also because evangelicals have invited it by their shortsighted opportunism and their lack of a coordinated impact whose deepest resources are spiritual and ethical.

However, God has not suspended the fate of the church in the world on American evangelicalism. It may well be that the evangelical church will rise to new spiritual power in unpredictable places and in ways that will avoid the weaknesses of contempory American evangelicalism. A new and spiritually renewed evangelicalism may, in fact, arise in America—one that drives the present evangelical powerbrokers to their knees.

Carl F.H. Henry talks about the challenge of critical thinking. In our last issue we announced the formation of the Christianity Today Institute. We have sensed the need for mature, scholarly thought applied to critical issues; the April 19 issue will include a major supplement from the institute's first meeting on "The Christian As Citizen."

Contributing to that meeting and the April supplement was Carl F.H. Henry. In light of his present and past experience with think tanks and their relationship to CT and the leadership community, we have interviewed him on the general subject of the need for broadly disseminated Christian thought.

Why We Need Christian Think Tanks
The Challenge of Critical Thinking

Q. How are the values and national goals of American society becoming restructured?
Dr. Henry. All the struts of civilized society seem to be giving way today, and the ferment in America is an aspect of that turmoil. The overarching question concerns the meaning and worth of human existence and survival; this embraces all the dilemmas of contemporary life, from the breakup of the family to abuse of drugs.

The church is affected because its families are affected. Humanism has penetrated education, the mass media, and politics, and it has debased God by insisting that he is irrelevant to the public realm. Further, much as it may at times be concerned to advance democracy, it has tended to underestimate the threat of totalitarian atheism.
Q. Is the church providing an adequate response?
A. If by adequacy we mean effective confrontation, the evangelical community tends to reduce its task in society to negation rather than recognizing the need to construct a full-orbed Christian alternative.
Q. How should evangelical thought leaders begin to shape an adequate response?
A. There are really three aspects to that: the place of evangelical thought leaders, the nature of a critical response, and the ways to affect society. At the outset, it should be said that conservative Christians have not esteemed their thinkers very highly. While we should honor those whose ministry is to put ideas into action, we must not devalue the intellectuals in the evangelical movement. Leadership is now too often identified with public activism, or entrepreneurial bigness, or mass media personality appeal.

Next, we must understand the nature of critical response. This is something more than hot rhetoric or the simplistic one-liner. We must honestly assess the alternatives being posed, identifying their weaknesses and inconsistencies, and also fairly representing their undesirable consequences. Beyond that, it is just as important to stipulate a clear and reasoned statement of a superior alternative that is obviously evangelical.

Finally, we must deal with two crucial aspects of how we can affect society. First, whatever needs to be said, we must say well. It is one thing to frame the problem and its answer correctly, but another to say it well. We must do this to gain a hearing. But, further, what we say needs to be heard where it most needs to be heard. Evangelicals tend to speak mostly to evangelicals rather than to the larger world.

Q. How can something like that be generated? Are action-oriented Christian groups filling the gap?

A. Lobbies are important, but they are weak apart from a comprehensive philosophy and strategy. The independent lobbies are mainly one-issue efforts that tend to exalt political clout above all other referents; sooner or later, political clout can be exercised by people on contrary sides of every subject. The answer needs to include the more reasoned efforts that address the issues; that means literature—books, journals, and articles that reach a secular audience.

Q. Many think tanks in Washington, D.C., analyze issues reflectively and suggest policy-setting priorities. Have evangelicals overlooked this possibility?

A. Evangelical think tanks have great potential if they are wisely conceived. Their agenda ought primarily to be set by the Bible. This means that a think tank aiming to serve the church will function Christianly if it presses the church to conform her agenda to the biblical mandate, and to rearrange her priorities properly. A competent think tank can raise the right questions and identify and reinforce right answers, but it will always be answerable to Holy Writ.

Q. A secular think tank is answerable mainly to the intellects involved in it. How would a Christian institute remain accountable to Scripture?

A. It will need theologians, philosophers, ethicists, lawyers, and politicians who seek above all else to be guided by scriptural concerns.

Q. So you think the term "think tank" suggests a useful approach in developing an evangelical response?

A. Yes, because the term "think tank," or perhaps "institute," is so broad it is very adaptable. On the scientific front, consider the Pasteur Institute formed in Paris almost a century ago. It produced magnificent results. Speaking generally, an institute exists for distinctive principles, and for either research, or study, or teaching, or communication associated with them. Many are identified with universities.

I have been related to three very different kinds. One is the Institute for Advanced Christian Studies. This was originally a fallback from hopes for a Christian university. It is now in the midst of producing a dozen books on issues relating Christianity to various disciplines.

A different type of institute is the Ethics and Public Policy Center in Washington. It has inner-city office space and workrooms, and a very competent intellectual at its helm. It has able research scholars and a highly trained office staff that produces books and pamphlets at the frontiers of contemporary social and political issues.

Another is the Institute for Religion and Democracy, also with a Washington base but much more modest quarters and limited staff. It functions well in dealing with issues of religious freedom, and with anxieties about Marxist penetration into Latin America.

Q. You participated in the first session of the Christianity Today Institute, which brought together J. I. Packer, Vernon Grounds, Nathan Hatch, Steven Monsma, David McKenna, and Myron Augsburger. When you were editor of *Christianity Today*, did you use the institute idea to bring together disparate points of view?

A. Yes and no. Years ago the Lilly Endowment gave *Christianity Today* $10,000 to gather about 20 outstanding evangelical scholars from secular universities. For three days we discussed the hindrances to evangelical faith on the secular campuses and how to address these in an intellectual and literary way. This significantly influenced the content of the magazine in the years that followed.

Q. In the church we have "practicing" leaders and "thought" leaders, though the two categories are not mutually exclusive. How do they need to inform one another?

A. Truth is Christianity's most enduring asset. When all other things—the picketing and the protesting—pass away, it is the question of the truth of Christianity that will ultimately determine its endurance. There are times indeed when Christians properly take to the streets. But the demand for political justice and social righteousness must not displace the mandate to evangelize, or the need for righteousness in personal or public life. Ideally, the life of every believer would be a blend of all the concerns of thought and action. Practicing leaders and thought leaders must work together to discover and proclaim that blend in light of today's particular pressures.

Q. In a sense, you and Billy Graham represent the "thought leader" and "practical leader" types. What would you say about the purpose and potential of the Christianity Today Institute?

A. In the last analysis, an evangelical institute will be known for some point of view that it thinks can give direction in the whole Christian mainstream. No institute is greater than the competence of its members to elaborate its principles. Also, granting that competence, its success will ultimately depend on how effectively it infuses its convictions throughout the social order.

Yet the reflective Christian will be especially aware that "we wrestle not against flesh and blood," but against the maddening misconceptions of a spiritually warped and morally malformed humanity. The apostle Paul, that great theologian-evangelist-social critic, reminds generation after generation that we contend against powers that require supernatural rebuttal, and without the Divine Superpower and our own comprehension of who the enemy truly is, all our efforts will be in vain.

The evangelists will have a way of keeping the institute on its knees and reminding those who participate in it of the indispensable mission to evangelize. The intellectuals can remind the evangelists that the task of the church is not one that neglects the course and fate of civilization. (*Christianity Today*, March 15, 1985.)

Carl F.H. Henry has had a long and distinguished career as an evangelical journalist and theologian. A founder of *Christianity Today* and its editor for many years, Dr. Henry now devotes much of his time to theological work. In this interview with freelance writer Wendy Lee Sereda, Dr. Henry talks about the role of Christianity in society today and in particular about the place of Christian journalism. Ms. Sereda lives in Palo Alto, California.

Talking with Carl Henry

Q. Is there a way for Christians to reform the mass media? Malcom Muggeridge suggests, for instance, that one should not even try to reform it.
Dr. Henry. I think we should use two strategies. I rather think that Malcolm Muggeridge overstates the gap between the secular media and the Christian potentialities. And even if the potentialities were minimal, we should exploit them. We should be there, penetrating. But on the other hand, we ought to develop our alternatives, and bring such competitive pressure on others that they will increasingly absorb, even if only out of sound financial instincts, the things that the Christian community is doing. Keep mounting the pressure, both ways. Beyond supporting our own alternatives, I believe we ought to be active in the public schools and PTA and support both. And not only merely support them in theory, but be out there knowing that as taxpayers we ought to have a voice in the public schools.
Q. So a brilliant film critique written for a religious magazine ought also to be submitted by the writer to newspapers in her area.
A. If she can get it published. Maybe the best she can do is to write a letter incorporating some of these criticisms and let the film editor respond. Or certain things can be said in a public letter to the editor. *There are always ways of getting a public hearing.*
Q. What is the responsibility of Christian journalism?
A. To set the movement of contemporary events in its moral and spiritual context, I presume, and to assess it in the light of the Christian view of history and its bearing on our time.
Q. How does that differ from secular journalism?
A. Secular journalism is more concerned merely to report the immediate pulsebeat of history. One frequent criticism of secular journalism today is that it tends only to reflect the culture rather than to pass a moral verdict on it. For that reason it is chaotic and easily caters to prurient interests.

Q. Are you in favor of a highly diversified series of journals with individual Christian perspectives, so that every Christian group can make its own statements?
A. Yes. Even modern philosophy, although it lacks a comprehensive world and life view in the main, tends increasingly to be occupied with the question of moral values in the different fields of learning. Christianity ought, however, to give some guidance concerning how one discriminates between competitive conceptions of the good. Then too, though modern reporting tends to be increasingly investigative, everybody is to be investigated but the press! Fortunately, the misguided Pulitzer Prize award to the *Washington Post* has tended to dispel that illusion slightly. The press is not the ultimate judge of our society, in the sense that it is immune from judgment for what itself does. What we desperately need today are just judges and just laws and a fair and discerning press.
Q. What is a fair press?
A. A press that does not try to prejudice the facts. I don't mean that there ought not to be columnists with divergent opinions. But when facts are so weighted as to reinforce the prejudiced views of the writers, I think that goes beyond the pale of exemplary journalism.
Q. Do you find, as I do, that leftist Christian journalism is polemical?
A. Journalism can be polemical both on the right and on the left, but I do think that the left often tends to prejudge events. For example, when I was in Johannesburg, I turned on my radio and heard that John Kennedy had been murdered. The very first report over the BBC was that the assassination was being attributed to right-wing influences opposed to Kennedy's civil rights program. As it later turned out, the facts were exactly the opposite. Lyndon Johnson always suspected that the Marxists had something to do with it.
Q. How, then, can a religious journal give leadership to the Christian community?
A. By identifying the crucial issues, by illuminating the problems posed by them, and by stating the values and limits of each approach to resolving them. Finally, it should give some constructive indication of where the editors stand and why.

The choice of events a journal covers and how it handles its coverage are critical as well. That is, in coverage of news events, the question must arise for a good evangelical editor how this event significantly bears on the frontier between church and world. Though all events take place in the full stream of history to which God is related, a news event of special significance to Christians would be one which bears on the fortunes of the church, or some aspect of it, in a significant way.

Q. What is the responsibility of the *reader* to whom the journal is giving leadership?

A. The reader should feel motivated to be more than a spectator, but to thrust himself or herself into the arena of ideas and values and to count publicly in some way—not vocally and verbally only but in other ways also.

Q. The first thing that I usually try to do as writer is to make the reader feel guilty in order to motivate him. How can I avoid that?

A. A better way, I think, would be to inspire him so that he drools to do something about it. So many areas are neglected today that I suppose the negative approach has its place. But evangelicals will really be strongest when they respond not out of a sense of guilt, but out of a real vision of a better alternative. The neglected frontiers really represent the golden opportunities.

Q. What neglected frontiers do you have a vision for?

A. I think often as an academician, of course. And I have wondered why evangelical colleges have emphasized for a whole generation that they articulate a Christian world and life view, in contrast to the modern outlook on life, when they have not taken the opportunity cooperatively to sponsor at least one film series of a Sunrise Semester type on the television stations right across America. The humanists from New York University can televise what humanism is all about. The Consortium of Evangelical Colleges and other cooperative efforts of these institutions have faculty resources and a generation-long dedication to the Christian world and life view. It seems incredible to me that they have not gotten together to present it in a way that would make it compelling to the secular world.

Then, too, the production of textbooks which present

Christian scholarship in a constructive and forceful way is too much neglected. The Institute for Advanced Christian Studies is now undertaking a series of books along this line.

Q. What is that?

A. IFACS is not a "buildings" project, but has a mobile base and is using its funds to undergird this series of college level texts by evangelical professors who are mostly on mainline university faculties.

I should also think that instead of each of the evangelical seminaries putting out its own journal, something might be gained if they would explore the possibility of putting the best of their scholarship in a common journal that could address the issues spoken to by all the seminaries in our day. There may be reasons why this isn't feasible, but it seems to me that here is a frontier opportunity.

Q. Do you think it appropriate to have a journal covering each of the areas of life—for instance, a journal on the relation of faith and art?

A. Yes, I think that is legitimate. Growing interest in each of the disciplines requires a sharing of perspectives and convictions.

Q. Would the Christian public at large read it?

A. I should think the readers would be students who are interested in the field, then the professionals who are leaders in it; for readership beyond that some clever editing would be needed. If the first article of every issue were to address art and its implications in its cultural context along with a Christian assessment and a discussion of the possibility of Christian alternatives, that would be one way to do it.

Q. Many articles in religious publications seem to be sermons on paper. How do you avoid that?

A. It takes time to do it creatively and interestingly. I find some good writing in the *New Oxford Review*, articles that are exceedingly well done, and in reading them I say, I wish I had done that, or could do it. It takes time.

A. Where does one find good writing outside of religious publications?

A. I don't always agree with them, but I'm impressed with the lucidity and the analytic skill of some of the editorial writers in our great daily papers, with some of the columnists and writers in *The American Scholar*, *Atlantic*, and other magazines. A lot can be learned from them. It seems to me that the editorials of many Christian journals are rather weak. *Christianity Today* has improved considerably in that area; *Eternity* runs some good copy.

Q. What makes a good editorial?

A. A good editorial lays bare the formative issues and analyzes what is to be said on both sides and then gives some constructive guidance. But it does all this with a literary flair—readability—that pulls the reader along, even when he or she may not want to think that strenuously.

Q. What is a good book review, as opposed to a good editorial?

A. A reviewer is presumed to be competent in the field, and may be expected to give a concluding verdict on whether this is a genuinely creative contribution or perhaps to suggest some better approach. The review, however, ought not to be primarily an expression of the reviewer's outlook on life, but rather an authentic portrayal of what the author is trying to say and how well he does it.

Q. What schools can you recommend that would teach writers to do this?

A. In our media-oriented age I would encourage every student who goes to college to take at least one course in journalism and in creative writing, even if one ends up able to do nothing more than post a letter to the editor! In that event at least the editorial page is not abandoned to radicals. But if one is going into a professional career, one ought to consider the great secular schools of journalism, for instance Medill, to learn the techniques and come to know others who across the years will be co-workers in the field. Then one has built-in ties and contacts. Though I never attended a secular school of journalism, I taught journalism at an evangelical college and taught religious journalism at several. I learned by experience. I'm sure that if I had gone to a secular school of journalism, I'd be a better writer. I did take courses in fiction writing, but never did much with it.

Q. Many of the readers of religious magazines are Christian students. How would you exhort them in their reading habits?

A. First, read, read, read. Read the classics. Read worthy bestsellers. Read "the best 20 books of the year," suggested by the annual lists that *Christianity Today* and *Eternity* put out, particularly the ones most important for one's own speculization—not necessarily what one agrees with, but what is being said in one's field. For many years I read a book a week; now I read more here and there.

Q. I heard you remark that my generation is guilty of "evangelical breastbeating." I think that is a fair assessment. Could you elaborate?

A. It is true that I think that one difference between evangelicals today and my own generation of young evangelicals is that those today tend to be more critical of the evangelical movement than of the world in general and society at large. In this way they reflect the tendency also of some of the evangelicals of the political left who were more critical of American involvement in Vietnam than they were of the forces who had initiated the conflict and of the predatory powers in modern history. There is more a call for pacifism at home than a condemnation of aggression abroad. That bothers me. I find it even worse when within the evangelical movement the church is blamed for all the ills of the world. Even if the church were nonexistent, the world would be blameworthy for the ills it has invited upon itself and the decisions it has refused to make, as well for wrong choices it has made.

I was in a church yesterday which joined in a resolution condemning Christian racial prejudice in another city where a congregation sold its building, not to blacks who offered $150,000 more, but to whites who offered less. Now that is deplorable. But the resolution went on to imply that the church is the main instrument of racial animosity and injustice in the world. Why not note that racial antagonisms and discrimination cling to the spirit of man in universal degeneracy and that it is all the more deplorable when the church, which is indeed an international and super-racial community, goes into debt to wicked worldy attitudes? That is quite another thing from blaming the church for the ailments of the world.

Q. Lifestyle is a priority issue for my generation. How can young people communicate to their parents and their churches in a gracious way?

A. As I see the lifestyle issue, a fundamental thing is the mindset and approachability of the Christian as a person. I don't think any staggering difference between "haves" and "have nots" is going to compensate for the lack of simple Christian gentility and approachableness. Lifestyle begins there—when a person is a person among persons. I don't like to see it shifted only to the world of things and away from interpersonal attitudes and relationships, so that the first question is, "What kind of car do you have?" or "What things do you have?" Secondly, I am convinced that it is not what people have but how they use what they have, what they do with it—whether they use it to the glory of God and in the service of their fellow humans—that is of first importance.

Q. Can a Christian journalist judge how they use possessions?
A. I think it is for God to judge, not for the Christian journalist to judge. I think that the Christian journalist should espouse the principles that are at stake, formulating them as clearly as possible. There may be helpful illustrations of funds used for God and for good, and vice-versa. It might be interesting to ask where the funds came from in the inaugurating of many Christian institutions. The list of evangelical philanthropists in this century is a glory gallery all of its own.

I am wholly convinced that Jesus meant serious business when he said that his disciples were not to live as the pagans do; that they were not to be known by the pursuit of affluence or things. At the same time, I think we ought to flee a sort of fundamentalist negation that judges in advance what lifestyle implies for Christian possessions universally. Let me illustrate that. I am a creative writer. I have a few beautiful oil paintings and antiques. I could get along without them. But they do something for me. When I see that an artist has made an idea powerfully attractive, it stimulates me conceptually and supplies motivations and aspirations for creative work. It is nobody's business that I got the paintings as originals in Amsterdam painted for those very frames, and that neither of those paintings cost me more than $60 or $75 at the time. But even if I had paid what they are worth today—which is plenty—they might well be justified in my type of work, even if some monastics might consider them a dispensable luxury. One has to make decisions before God in this matter. The real question is, What does one *do* with what he or she has? Things are an entrustment. Abraham was wealthy and the Bible says God loved him; wealth brings problems that I have never had to face, but the Bible does not view it as an evil.

I don't think the problem of poverty will be solved either by a global evangelical handout or by a bureaucratic redistribution of wealth. But I think evangelical voluntarism is a test of sensitivity to Christian imperatives and a witness to the truth of God. Some of our Christian causes would be better off if some Christians *were* more prosperous and had more to give. The great day of Christian philanthropy in some ways seems to be vanishing as Big Brother taxes it away and presumes to be a cosmic Santa Claus.

On the other hand, the lifestyle issue is a real one, one that needs to be pressed today, because many in the churches have been infected by worldly values and by materialistic longings. That probably doesn't have enough bite for you; nevertheless, that is the way I feel about it!

Q. There always seems to be a theory/practice gap when it comes to lifestyle, doesn't there?

A. Yes. For instance, American liberals who were all for public schools and resisted any serious critique of them—the Kennedy group—placed their own children in private schools. There's something curious about a program of political criticism that exempts oneself from the principles projected on others.

Q. Do you think that Christian journals can fight for their fair share against the burgeoning economic interest by Christians in other media areas? Is there a future for the printed word?

A. I think there will always be a place for the printed word. I think the printed word is somehow materialized and planted in history in a way in which the other media programs are not. Radio and television programs are under immediate program pressures that cancel viewer impressions, while printed material has a built-in possibility of permanence.

Q. What can fill the gap between purely devotional books and issue-oriented books which are no more than a string of Bible verses on issues?

A. I think we must see an awakening of theological interest if the "evangelical awakening" is really to take root and if the political engagement of the evangelicals is to find the direction it really needs; some wrestling of Christian social ethics in a more earnest and more comprehensive way is also needed. There has been too much interest in personal adventure themes ("I was a drug addict," etc.). The evangelical book clubs have found more interest in this than in more worthy material. In a way, I have been fortunate that my own work, *God, Revelation and Authority*, has gone into a third English printing. I think the time is ripe. Young evangelical students on the campuses are getting more seriously interested in the world of ideas. The interest of non-Christians is in jobs and dollars more than in ideas and service. I think that young evangelicals increasingly realize that any "taking of the future" must involve familiarity with the war in the world of ideas and a lively engagement in the conflict.

An exclusive interview with Dr. Carl F.H. Henry by two editors, Edward Rowe and David Juroe of "Applied Christianity." Dr. Henry is one of America's leading evangelical scholars and spokesmen.

Christianity and Government

Q. Dr. Henry, I believe I read somewhere that you were quoted as stating that there are some 42 million evangelical Christians in our country.
Dr. Henry. That sounds right. When I edited *Christianity Today*, we ran a check in 1967 that left no doubt that the evangelical Christians are the largest segment of the American religious spectrum. If one puts together the conservative evangelicals within the National Council of Churches, other bodies that are predominantly evangelical like the Southern Baptists, Missouri-Synod Lutherans and the Third Force churches, those affiliated with the National Association of Evangelicals, the American Council of Churches, and many others without any ecumenical identification, evangelicals far outnumber non-evangelicals in the American religious community.
Q. Let's take the figure of 42 million. Do you have any idea what percentage of these people are active Christians? First of all, active in the personal, spiritual dimensions of the Christian life, and secondly, in the church life and thirdly, what percentage of these people might be active in some way in the application of Christianity in society?
A. Those are highly interesting questions. Because of their confidence in Scripture as the written Word of God, evangelicals are certainly most interested in the faithful reading and distribution of the Scriptures. To what extent they are involved in the social and public arena is another question. Certain individuals have been involved in public life at various levels, and some evangelical denominations more than others emphasize the importance of public involvement. In the last ten or fifteen years there has been a growing conviction that evangelicals have neglected a necessary involvement in the public arena.

Q. Dr. Henry, approximately two years ago you wrote a book entitled *A Plea for Evangelical Demonstration* in which you urged evangelicals to become involved in some of the major issues of the day—social issues and other such issues. Do you feel that the book has been well received among evangelicals? Have Christian people read the book with understanding and paid attention to its message?

A. Well, ever since I wrote the *Uneasy Conscience of Modern Fundamentalism* in the late 1940's, when an emphasis on evangelical social involvement was rather unpopular, there has been a growing awareness on the part of the evangelical community that it was not adequately and ideally related to the world at large. Had I not gone to *Christianity Today* at its founding, I would have shaped the major work on Christian social ethics alongside my *Christian Personal Ethics*. I have two or three steel file drawers full of partly completed chapters and lecture notes that will never see daylight simply because of other priorities. So I have had to content myself with occasional lectures such as those reprinted in *Aspects of Christian Social Ethics* and *A Plea for Evangelical Demonstration*. These emphases are getting a hearing, whether through these particular books or the extension of the same ideas in other ways. I firmly believe that ideas have consequences, and one idea that needs desperately to be heard today is the burning necessity for a demonstration of evangelical conviction in all the arenas of modern life.

Q. As you know, Dr. Henry, we're at a moment in history which is referred to by many people as the "Watergate era." I'm wondering what in your opinion is the effect of this on the evangelical mind? Do you feel that evangelicals are disillusioned in general and dropping out of the system? Or do you feel that they're recognizing a vacuum into which Christianity must move if we're going to save the country and maintain our freedoms?

A. The reaction to Watergate can be measured in numerous ways. In Latin America and elsewhere abroad there was evident reaction. Many foreigners felt that Americans should not have been surprised by Watergate because they expect governments to be corrupt. I believe that many evangelicals were stunned by Watergate because many of them, like myself, had

Christianity and Government 177

higher expectations from the present leadership. At the time of President Nixon's election, I wrote a front page editorial for a British magazine stating that many Americans expected a deeper commitment to moral and spiritual priorities during the Nixon era. President Johnson had been more or less of an ecumenical "round about" and had not put down deep church roots. But when an adminstration stressing law and order was overtaken by massive compromises and illegalities, the disillusionment ran through evangelical as well as nonevangelical ranks. This has shaped disenchantment over the American political processes and to some extent also over the mass media as charges of irresponsibility fly back and forth. This disenchantment is fed by political opponents of the present administration, and of course, also by opponents of capitalism and free enterprise who indict the American system as itself unjust. The tragic thing is that such criticisms are made more and more in the absence of any commitment to noble alternatives, although public figures of integrity stand tall in times like these, even if most publicity goes to the seamy side. Here is where an opportunity faces the evangelical community. We should be channeling into politics and into all the arenas of American life young leadership that is vocationally competent and dedicated to Christian principles.

Q. Do you feel that there is a pervading mood developing among evangelicals regarding these alarming trends? Do people think that no changes are possible—that Christian participation in the political and social process is out of the question because Christians can't change the country no matter how much they try?

A. Some persons are dropping out, especially many in the Jesus-movement who as part of the counter-cultural revolt were turned off by the establishment, although many of these are simply waiting for "the system" to fall apart through inner weaknesses. But today many evangelicals are convinced that precisely the *absence* of adequate evangelical participation has accommodated a deterioration of public morality on the American scene. I know many young evangelicals are going into law and are looking at the political arena with greater interest, although they cross their fingers because of the financial expense of mounting a political career.

Q. APPLIED CHRISTIANITY is vitally interested in encouraging Christian participation in the democratic process. In your opinion, does Christian civic responsibility have a clear scriptural basis?

A. It has indeed a scriptural basis. I am not thinking here of translating Christianity into civil religion, although no nation escapes some form of civil religion, and it is senseless to let non-Christians shape the national milieu without challenge. The key passage is Romans 13. The problem of an adequate relating of personal religion and public issues is one that existed already in the Old Testament period when the kings of Israel ventured treaties with powerful neighbor-nations and neglected personal religion. The prophets had to remind both the king and people that the nation was headed for calamity without obedience to the will of God in public life and without personal faith in Yahweh. In the New Testament, in the absence of a theocracy, the problem is somewhat the opposite. The New Testament Christians knew themselves to be twice born men and women constituting a new society called out of the world but sent back into it again for a special mission. In the 13th chapter of Romans, Paul says that God wills government in our fallen society for the preservation of justice and for the restraint of disorder, and that Christians have an obligation to support such government for conscience sake. We ought to seek through government as an instrumentality of justice what God wills in the way of universal justice.

Q. Dr. Henry, do you feel that some of the evangelicals today, especially among the intelligentsia, are accepting Marxist panaceas for the ills of our society and if so why?

A. Marxism is, of course, a broad term. No evangelicals are accepting Marxism as an atheistic philosophy. If you mean Marxism, as economic philosophy, this has become attractive to some evangelicals in Latin America especially. Part of the reason is that in a land where 80% of the people are declared to be still in poverty after 400 years of Roman Catholicism and 100 years of Protestant missions, some evangelicals are looking elsewhere for economic answers. Since Marxists alone seem to be speaking to the social predicament, it is to Marxist alternatives that people tend to rally. That's why I think the time has come when evangelicals need to formulate social criticism

Christianity and Government 179

in a more acceptable framework. Marxism raises some of the right questions but gives wrong answers. The right questions originated elsewhere. The Marxist concern for the poor and the afflicted and vision of a coming utopia is borrowed, even is seriously distorted, from the Bible.

I think evangelicals need to say even more insistently than Marxists that it is unjust for a half million people living in Lima, Peru, to live in cardboard huts in 55 degree weather seeking to eke out a miserable survival winter after winter. We ought to speak up on behalf of the destitute who have such minimal survival needs as clothing and shelter. We need to be concerned when human beings do not have work that offers some promise of coping with basic needs and of lifting human existence to a plane of meaningful survival. If we can't help to create situations in which jobs are a possibility—voluntarily if possible, which is the preferable way—we've got to look for other ways of helping them on a temporary basis. One costly turn in American life came with the 1929 depression when voluntary agencies were unable to cope with the massiveness of the problems. Thereafter, a temporary government intervention came to be accepted as the permanent ideal.

Q. Should the church support legislative measures?
A. In the case of Hitler, there was every need for the institutional church to speak out. But it is wholly untenable to make his extreme situation a precedent for the church to be involved in the day-to-day legislative positions and political commitments. In recent years we have seen an effort to mount political pressure in the name of the church for specific legislative positions. I think this is lamentable from two points of view. First, the legitimacy of the espoused positions was often in doubt, so that the churches became polarized in two different camps depending upon the stance taken by denominational or ecumenical leaders. Secondly, it was seldom clear how these social or political pronouncements were derived from the Bible itself, though promulgated in the name of Christ, the church, the cross or Christian ethics.

Q. How should our elected officials perceive the relationship between God and government?
A. I believe that when a president speaks in his role as the leader of the people, he will ideally speak theistically. I think

that government under God is the only legitimate government. President Eisenhower set a good example for us in this regard. I have regarded President Nixon as much too cautious about using the name of God in public address, although this side of the Watergate trouble it's probably too late to encourage a meaningful alteration of emphasis.

Q. Do you see a need for broad-based activity among evangelical Christians nationally—activity designed to encourage Christian participation in the American system?

A. It seems to me that all evangelical Christians ought to be engaged in the political process to the fullest measure of their competence and ability.

Q. In your estimation does consistent Biblical Christianity necessarily lead an individual to a conservative viewpoint on political and social issues?

A. The term "conservative viewpoint" is very ambiguous, for it represents quite a spectrum of commitment. Over and against the pragmatic orientation of a liberal viewpoint, which seems to lack commitment to fixed principles, a commitment in terms of controlling principles has more in common with a biblical perspective. Moreover, the attack on the legitimacy of private property and of the profit motive by radically leftist ideologies has no real biblical grounding. The Bible itself is critical of the misuse of property and possessions, and the abuse of the principle of profit. There is an ongoing effort on the part of some, however, to justify communism in terms of a New Testament precedent. But it has no adequate basis. The Apostle Paul never enjoined community of goods for Christian believers as a criterion of their commitment to Christ. The Jerusalem church practiced community possessions only for a short time and did so voluntarily. This one church, curiously, was in financial difficulty on-goingly because Paul seems frequently to be taking collections for the poor believers in Jerusalem.

Q. Dr. Henry, a current scholar, Dr. David Moberg, has come out with a book entitled *The Great Reversal*, in which he claims that initially most of the great social institutions of America were founded by Christian private charity or Christian organizations. But in this century there has been a reversal whereby evangelicals no longer are very much involved in

Christianity and Government 181

social issues. Do you believe the reason for the reversal is that noninvolvement is an over-reaction to the Social Gospel viewpoint which would do violence to the correct Scriptural perspective on Christian social activity?

A. Yes, evangelicals over-reacted to the Social Gospel. The Social Gospel was a philosophy of social concern mounted on three premises. First, it was an anti-miraculous philosophy of religion which ignored transcendent revelation and divinely-provided salvation. Second, it assumed that utopian social situation cold be achieved without a supernatural rebirth of sinners; it viewed man as secretly divine. Thirdly, it regarded history as automatically moving towards utopia and thought this developing process could be facilitated by commitment to socialist, and in some cases, to communist ideals. So evangelicals rightly reacted against a non-biblical world view, but they over-reacted in concentrating on evangelism and missions to the neglect of public responsibility. That stance was very different from the attitude in 18th Century Britain when the evangelical awakening spared England from the throes of the French Revolution. At that time, evangelicals who firmly believed in the necessity of the new birth and in the biblical view of man and redemption, were at the same time in the forefront of social concern and took an initiative with regard to illiteracy, poverty, education of the poor, improved factory conditions, improved prison condition, child labor laws, indignation in the face of slavery and so on.

Q. Do you feel that the evangelical theological seminary has a legitimate role as a training school for Christian involvement in the political-social realm or should it stick merely to biblical theology, per se?

A. I think personal and social ethics has a legitimate place in our seminaries. But schools often get young professors, who having recently taken their doctorates in universities, tend to come out uncritically on the liberal left. If evangelical Christians were to pour their energies into their churches and their communities in terms of an exemplary Christian commitment and involvement, this nation could still see better days than in its highest hours of the past. That will not come about without a new commitment on the part of the evangelical community itself. We must become aware of past inadequacies and awaken to a new sensitivity and possibilities of renewal in the life of the nation. Evangelical Christians need to become politically involved at the precinct level as an expression of their social duty. There is no reason in all of this for a neglect of biblical theology and of evangelistic concern in the seminaries, as if one must choose between evangelism and politics. God purposes certain objectives through the church and certain objectives through civil government. His followers have no license to neglect one or the other.

Carl F.H. Henry is respected as the dean of American evangelical theologians. Since 1974 he has been a lecturer at large for World Vision, an interdenominational world mission organization. This assignment has taken him to the farthest reaches of the globe to speak at theological schools.

Dr. Henry has held professorial rank at four American seminaries. He was first editor of *Christianity Today*, which began publication in 1956. He served as chairman of the World Congress on Evangelism in Berlin in 1966.

Among the 23 books he has written are *Remaking the Modern Mind, Aspects of Christian Social Ethics*, and *The Biblical Expositor*. He was editor of *Baker's Dictionary of Christian Ethics*.

These days he is well along in his *magnum opus*, a four-volume theological treatise entitled *God, Revelation and Authority*, the first two volumes of which have been published by Word.

For Dr. Henry's perspective on the state of Christianity, *Christian Herald* editors talked with him at his home in Arlington, Virginia.

Where the Church Stands

Q. Dr. Henry, much has been made of the great number of Americans who regard themselves as evangelical or born-again Christians, yet signs seem to point to continuing moral decay in our land. How do you account for this and when do you think the current revival will begin to have a more significant impact upon behavior?

Dr. Henry. The evangelical surge in America is a remarkable phenomenon. From the 40-45 million evangelicals numbered in the 1960s, George Gallup—who now counts himself an evangelical Episcopalian—estimates 50 million who today consider themselves "born again." Some venture to say that, counting evangelical Catholics and Jews, and all varieties of charismatics, their number is still greater.

In the early 1940s nobody wanted the label "evangelical"; modernism and then neoorthodoxy were the vogue. The National Association of Evangelicals, flashing an explicit doctrinal statement, garnered 1,800,000 members; yet here is a tide of 40-million-plus. Seeking to control or to capture this phenomenon is like trying to catch a space satellite in a butterfly net, even if some groups may maneuver to do so.

One danger is that the promotion of cooperation only for purposes of evangelistic utility will confuse the already muddled masses. Another is that an evasion of doctrinal concerns will simply postpone division to a more costly future. Yet there surely are legitimate areas of evangelical cooperation that need not involve detailed doctrinal consensus. National concerns are a significant example—protesting the wrong, promoting and defining the right, exemplifying the good and the godly, struggling for justice, supporting and providing proper leadership, and so on.

Insofar as people perceive themselves as evangelicals while they use the term *reborn* only of long-past experiences that carry no vital import for present living, or while they invoke the authority of Scripture only in an inconsistent or broken way, their need for a deepening of ties to Christ and the Bible is apparent. Those who are counted in evangelistic crusades as having "raised hands" and "decided" for Christ must be considered in a doubtful class unless they become openly aligned with other Christians in evangelical outreach, for on any other basis they appear stillborn and remain part of the problem rather than the answer.

A sign of traditional "evangelical awakening" lies in the impact of Christian verities and values on the public mind and conscience. The unembarrassed moral decay and spiritual sloth of masses of Americans, the basically antisupernatural stance of university learning, and the catering of the media to modern permissiveness all indicate areas that call for constructive evangelical challenge and engagement.

Q. What message or messages do you think God wants American Christians to hear now?

A. We need a vision of the transcendent holiness of God. The whole climate of American life tends to work against an awareness of God's holiness. The destruction of a million fetuses in a single year can't be dismissed as simply a personal matter. It says something about the nation and its attitudes. So do the breakdown of the family and the easy tolerance of divorce, the breakdown of the nuclear family, the accommodation of the churches to the culture, so that they are only five or ten years behind the frontier permissive movements.

I myself am not ready to say we are in the midst of an evangelical awakening. I think the media have begun, not simply to reflect the evangelical momentum of the recent past, but also to trivialize the evangelical mentality and outlook. "Born again" is used for the remodeling of a shopping center. If the media were to revert—as well they may within a short time—to the Elmer Gantry era, we would find ourselves in a highly defensive role.

We need to proclaim that all things may be new, across the board. The messages that currently draw the largest crowds and appear to have greatest outward success appeal to the latent potential in individuals, yet I think God will support and prosper the proclamation of the message of his holiness. The missing note in much of American preaching is a calling of public conscience to God's standards and God's criteria. I don't think we've had since Walter Maier someone who spoke to the conscience of American people outside of churches. Until American's begin to judge themselves by God's commandments they will continue to accommodate to permissiveness.

Q. To what extent does the church today draw its agenda of issues and concerns from the world?

A. All too much. Ideally the church draws her concerns from the Bible and sets the issues in view of the world's priorities. The danger is that the world will needlessly be given the initiative—first in stipulating priorities, then in defining their nature, and finally in excluding all else as marginal, optional or irrelevant. The church is against the world, in the world, and for the world—in that order; it is the one community that owes its origin, nature and task in the world to the crucified and risen Christ. But the world gets all too easily into the church. In our day ecumenism faltered because the world too often set its agenda, and evangelical churches of whatever alignment will fail God and the world if they repeat the same mistake.

Q. How do you view the movement to ordain homosexuals as ministers?

A. Homosexuality calls both for compassionate understanding and for moral censure; the Bible asks for repentance and discontinuance. Whatever elements of heredity and environment may encourage it, God knows also the elements of responsible voluntary decision that enter into its practice. A church that ordains homosexuals may next consider ordaining prostitutes also; once confessional and ethical beliefs are culturally oriented, the sky is the limit. When the apostle Paul wrote the Corinthian believers—"... such were some of you. But you were washed, you were sanctified, you were justified in the name of the Lord Jesus Christ," I Cor. 6:11—he had in view homosexual offenders as well as other sexual deviants. If homosexuals are banned from Christian circles, they are excluded from the only redemptive society that can truly help them. But there is little help either to God's cause or to man's in conferring ordination on inordinancy.

Q. It would be tempting to find the explanation only in "society" or in "the cultural drift." But the root problem lies even more deeply in the human person. The appalling wickedness of mankind underlies the moral revolt and spiritual indifference everywhere, and Satan and all the forces of evil nourish it. This depravity is as bad in Western culture, and perhaps more so, than elsewhere, since the West has been the greatest beneficiary of the Great Commission, of the best as well as the worst in the medieval heritage, and the Protestant Reformation.

It has turned against light; atheism now rules officially where churches once prevailed, and radical secularism abounds where the Reformation once thrived. The universities stifle faith in God, revealed truths and divine commandments, and the mass media—television especially—reinforce the impression that biblical beliefs and values are archaic, while some political and business tycoons exploit religious image as much as some others call for spiritual reality. Worse yet, evangelical forces concentrate on evangelistic emphases so onesidedly that they have no effective strategy for boldly penetrating the cultural milieu. Instead, they tend to forsake it by exploiting fears and establishing new and larger ghettos.

Q. What in your view have been the most significant events of the twentieth century?

A. Two world wars erupting in the so-called Christian West, the last of which frustrated the global ambitions of German and Japanese militarists; the rise of atheistic Communism as a world force; the scientific thrust into the air, nuclear and space-age and the genetic breakthrough; the emergence and declension of Protestant ecumenism and the crisis of authority in the Church of Rome; the emergence of the United Nations and its ineffectiveness in crisis-times; the ballooning of the utopian pretensions of secular democracy, Communism and socialism and their costly consequence in a loss of faith in social institutions; the third world overconfidence in the ultimate political solution of all problems, and the reentry of mainland China into the world political arena; the regathering of Jewry to Palestine and formation of the nation Israel, and the world energy crisis magnifiying the steady acceleration of evangelical Christianity amid the rise and decline of modernism and neoorthodoxy and radical secularism; the swift decline of money-and sex-oriented Western culture and appearance of countercultural youth; the soaring worldwise inflationary spiral, and the breakdown of family values in a relapse to pagan immorality in erstwhile Christian lands; the rise and trivialization of the mass media; and the moral and intellectual failure of the great universities and emergence despite them of a vigorous Christian youth movement.

Q. Some critics say that no hard evidence exists that our generation is morally worse than earlier generations, and that only religious pessimists talk about the collapse of Western culture. What do you make of that?

A. Arnold Toynbee and other historians depict the doom of every past civilization, and ours is in line. Each civilization doubtless had its soothsayers who prattled about utopian perpituity. To be sure, the modern West's most sordid aspects are no worse than ancient Sodom and Gomorrah or Pompeii, if that holds any comfort. But even responsible scientists and philosophers speak of the looming end of our age, whether in terms of overpopulation and famine, or of possibilities of nuclear destruction or ecological pollution.

Theologians and evangelists keep in view the end of all ends, or God's final moral and spiritual judgment of men and nations. Those who say "matters are not worse" often lack any fixed ethical norm and regard human behavior as merely culture-relative. In regard to the scriptural standards there can be little doubt that two developments are under way. Multitudes whose biblical ties are shallow are being uprooted by the wild winds of modernity that carry them like tumbleweeds into every dark and devious corner.

At the same time a growing evangelical vanguard, for whom secular life had turned sour, is finding God and the faith of the Bible to be real and vital. The United States is currently in a historic decision time that could shape national attitudes either way for the rest of this century.

Q. What doctrine currently negelcted by the Christian church needs most to be reproclaimed today and why?

A. I don't much believe in the notion that different biblical doctrines need special emphasis in successive historical ages. All biblical doctrines need to be proclaimed as a coherent unity. The Christian world-life view should be set persuasively over against its modern rivals. In all ages the authority and reliability of the Bible deserves full emphasis; if inspired Scripture is untrustworthy in its teaching, then the doctrines it teaches have no higher status than other human conjecture and theory. Faced by the tawdry morality of this age, Christians daily need the Holy Spirit's fullness. All signs point, moreover, to the rise of new conflict over christology, and the Christian doctrine of God will be increasingly in debate. We shall need most of all to exhibit a full-orbed biblical theology.

Q. Your style of commentary tends to be polemical, although you are usually very gentle in your argumentation. Would you say that this style arose out of the time in which you lived with the modernist-fundamentalist controversy? Does our day still call for such an apologetic or might it be structured along more positive lines?

A. My aim from the outset has been a positive thrust. I've talked face to face, and in a gentlemanly way, with scores of philosophers and theologians of divergent views. Sound argument needs always to be fashioned with precision and to be stated pointedly; all the devices of logic—including the appeal to a man's heart as well as his mind—are appropriate. An effective evangelical apologetic will always include both internal and external criticism of other views. But truth and love belong together, and I trust I have not been loveless toward those whom I would persuade, for my mind and heart go out to them, and I am aware of my own finiteness and vulnerability.

Q. You tend to urge sharp distinctions between evangelism and education. Can either be left wholly to specialists? Don't all Christians have certain obligations in both areas?

A. Of course, I have had a 40-year stake in both education and evangelism. But Christians must not expect all ends from every means. The public schools are not to be used as instruments of evangelism either by theists or by humanists, who tend presently to crowd the minds of students. And the home and the church have high educational duties as well as evangelistic duties.

I think a wave of disenchantment with university and college education is in the making, and that new alternatives will appear. But Christianity has a deep stake in the liberal arts and in all cultural interests, and this is precisely the time to encourage collegians to pursue the highest degrees in their areas of competence and to permeate the world of learning with a comprehensive outlook that does not eclipse the reality of God, fixed truth and universal values.

Q. Many grassroots believers are discovering real fellowship with others of very different denominational backgrounds. Do you sense a gathering grassroots ecumenism that leaders have ignored?

A. I'm sure that's the case. There are probably tens of thousands of small neighborhood Bible study groups and prayer meetings. Here in the Washington area it's been going on ever since Key '73. How long it will last, we don't know.

The reason the chairs are here in a circle is that there are from 15 to 25 people who gather every other Friday in a home, on a mobile basis, and we'll meet tonight and study the last chapter of the book of Revelation. There are college students, homemakers, workers, professional people. Last time we met at the home of a member of the SALT commission.

One of the big things in Korea now, where there is great anxiety about the possibility of war, is that Christians, who are about 15 percent of the population, not only attend church regularly but also meet regularly in neighborhood groups on Friday evenings. Whatever happens, all the Christians will be known to each other.

Q. Any other thoughts about a distinctly Christian contribution to the current scene?

A. There's an absence of joy in comtemporary life. The gospel is among other things an infectious source of joy in a world pervaded by a sense of melancholy and gloom. I've always been impressed that Augustine, the great philosopher, even before he became a Christian, was impressed initially not by philosophical argument, although that came in its time, but by the spontaneous joy of the Christians he met.

Contemporary Christians need to understand again that joylessness is a sin. It betrays a great deal about the shallowness of spiritual experience when joy is absent. We in Western society tend to be preoccupied with material things which give us only a transient happiness, as it were, if indeed happiness is the term for it, but joy is something that has its roots in the transcendent world, surpassing anything material things can provide or take away.

SYMPOSIUM SERIES

1. Jurgen Moltman *et al.*, **Religion and Political Society**
2. James Grace, editor, **God, Sex, and the Social Project: The Glassboro Papers on Religion and Human Sexuality**
3. M. Darrol Bryant and Herbert Richardson, editors, **A Time for Consideration: A Scholarly Appraisal of the Unification Church**
4. Donald G. Jones, editor, **Private and Public Ethics: Tensions Between Conscience and Institutional Responsibility**
5. Herbert Richardson, editor, **New Religions and Mental Health: Understanding the Issues**
6. Sheila Greeve Davaney, editor, **Feminism and Process Thought: The Harvard Divinity School/Claremont Center for Process Studies Symposium Papers**
7. International Movement, A.T.D./Fourth World, **Children of Our Time: The Children of the Fourth World**
8. Jenny Hammett, **Woman's Transformations: A Psychological Theology**
9. S. Daniel Breslauer, **A New Jewish Ethics**
10. Darrell J. Fasching, editor, **The Jewish People in Christian Preaching**
11. Henry Vander Goot, **Interpreting the Bible in Theology and the Church**
12. Everett Ferguson, **Demonology of the Early Christian World**
13. Marcia Sachs Littell, editor, **Holocaust Education: A Resource Book for Teachers and Professional Leaders**
14. Char Miller, editor, **Missions and Missionaries in the Pacific**
15. John S. Peale, **Biblical History as the Quest for Maturity**
16. Joseph A. Buijs, editor, **Christian Marriage Today: Growth or Breakdown ?**
17. Michael Oppenheim, **What Does Revelation Mean for the Modern Jew?**
18. Carl F.H. Henry, **Conversations with Carl Henry: Christianity for Today**